Reculturing Schools as Professional Learning Communities

Jane Bumpers Huffman
Kristine Kiefer Hipp

With contributing authors Anita M. Pankake, Gayle Moller,
Dianne F. Olivier, and D'Ette Fly Cowan

ScarecrowEducation
Lanham, Maryland • Toronto • Oxford
2003

Published in the United States of America
by ScarecrowEducation
An imprint of The Rowman & Littlefield Publishing Group, Inc.
4501 Forbes Boulevard, Suite 200, Lanham, Maryland 20706
www.scarecroweducation.com

PO Box 317
Oxford
OX2 9RU, UK

British Library Cataloguing in Publication Information Available

Library of Congress Cataloging-in-Publication Data
Huffman, Jane Bumpers, 1950–
   Reculturing schools as professional learning communities / Jane
Bumpers Huffman, Kristine Kiefer Hipp.
      p. cm.
   "A ScarecrowEducation book."
   ISBN 1-57886-053-9 (pbk. : alk. paper)
   1. School improvement programs—United States. 2. Educational
change—United States. I. Hipp, Kristine Kiefer, 1949– II. Title.
LB2822.82.H84 2003
371.2—dc21   2003008250

♾️^{TM} The paper used in this publication meets the minimum requirements of
American National Standard for Information Sciences—Permanence of
Paper for Printed Library Materials, ANSI/NISO Z39.48-1992.
Manufactured in the United States of America.

We dedicate this book to Shirley M. Hord, for her vision and leadership in creating communities of learners. Dr. Hord's devotion to continuous learning and her numerous mentoring efforts have inspired her national and international colleagues and coworkers. On behalf of the many people Shirley has taught and influenced throughout her career, we offer our most sincere thanks and appreciation. We also dedicate this book to the outstanding educators who work tirelessly to provide opportunities for all children to succeed. We honor your contributions and support your continued work.

Contents

Foreword: Why Communities of Continuous Learners?

> Our work is not granted freely to human beings but must be adventured and discovered, cultivated and earned. It is the result of application, dedication, an indispensable sense of humor, and above all a never-ending courageous conversation with ourselves, those with whom we work, and those whom we serve.
>
> —David Whyte

A community of continuous learners—professional learners—is a key element of school capacity, a way of working, and the most powerful professional development and change strategy available for improving our educational system. When professionals, schoolwide, come together frequently and regularly to reflect on their practice, to assess their effectiveness, to collectively study in a social context what they consider to be areas in need of attention, and to make decisions about what they need to learn to become more effective, they are operating as a community of professional learners.

Such learners who are improving their schools include administrators and teachers of PreK–12 in public as well as private schools. Their *improvement* of practice is based on *change* of practice, and change of practice is based on *learning*. Change of knowledge, understanding, insights, skills, behaviors, attitudes, beliefs, and values requires learning. But where do the professionals, who are responsible and accountable for the ongoing reform and improvement of education that is offered to young children and to young adults, gain access to quality learning to support their responsibilities? In traditional schools, teachers aren't talking to other teachers, and schools aren't interacting with each other. The result is classrooms operating in isolation, with teaching all too often mundane, uninspiring, and lacking in intellectual rigor.

Although learning can take place with the individual in an independent setting, group or organizational learning in a social context provides a richer format in which information is processed; ideas are challenged; concepts are debated; and higher intellectual activity, based on the capacities of the individuals involved, is the result. Organizational learning does not embrace isolationism. On the contrary, it embraces professional learning communities where professionals work with and support each other as learners. In this book, we argue that organizational learning, or learning in a social context, is more effective than individual learning.

A BRIEF HISTORY OF EDUCATIONAL IMPROVEMENT

The Soviet Union's launch of *Sputnik* in the late fifties prompted the United States to question how it had fallen behind in the space program and stimulated a broad investigation of schooling in the United States. The result was the design and dissemination of a great deal of curriculum programs that would correct this situation, with the "alphabet" programs sent to public school teachers and to college preparatory courses. During this same time, theorists articulated change process models that described how change could happen. Prominent among these were Chin and Benne (1969) and Havelock (1971), followed later by House (1981) and Sashkin and Egermeier (1992), whose models shared overlapping conceptualizations. In one approach, these authors posit that if a "good" change were suggested, people of good intention would adopt the change and use it to good results.

However, if this approach were not adequate, then a second approach that relies on the additional factor of influencing individuals and systems to change through legislation and external power of various types (e.g., state legislative policies, superintendents' mandates) would be employed. History is replete with mandates and other power strategies that resulted in little change. Charters and Jones (1973) waggishly labeled the attention to such lack of results as an appraisal of nonevents. This foreword challenges the assumption that invoking policy mandates alone, albeit well intended and directed toward increasing success for all students, is enough to realize such outcomes as increased student success. Even though these approaches are used extensively to this day with little real effect, it is clear that they are inadequate, and that a different approach is necessary—an approach proposed by this book.

Beginning in the 1970s, a great deal of attention was given to the effective schools research and its related school improvement process. The "correlates of effective schools" provided the framework for many schools around the globe to think about and plan for school change (Edmonds, 1979; Lezotte & Bancroft, 1985). Evolving from this body of work came the emphasis of the importance of the school principal, whose actions were widely studied and reported, and were used as a means for addressing the reform of schools (Fullan, 1991; Hansen & Smith, 1989; Leithwood & Montgomery, 1982; Lieberman & Miller, 1981; Little, 1981; Mortimore & Sammons, 1987; Rutherford, Hord, Huling, & Hall, 1983; Thomas, 1978). And even though the principal's role has clearly remained a significant factor, the school's improvement is but one of many responsibilities of the principal.

In 1983, *A Nation at Risk* again lamented the poor state of schools, and much like the *Sputnik* era decades earlier, much activity ensued regarding what should happen to improve schools. Unfortunately, not much improvement resulted. More recently, in 1997 the U.S. Congress funded the comprehensive school reform demonstration (CSRD) program. Congress studied the evaluations of the billion-dollar investment in Title 1, with its disappointing results. Subsequently, legislation created the CSRD program. It was hypothesized that the money given to schools was not coupled with the school's sufficient knowledge and skills for employing the money meaningfully. Thus, Congress wrote legislation that required a school to adopt a research-based, results-proven program in order to be funded. Final outcomes of this approach to school reform are yet to be identified, but informal assessments indicate varying degrees of success.

This brief sketch highlighting aspects of school change and improvement history suggests the inadequacy of the approaches noted here. In this book we offer a different, and quite necessary, approach.

A NEW APPROACH

In the 1980s, in public education and in the corporate world, attention began to focus on how work settings influenced workers. *Corporate Cultures* by Deal and Kennedy (1982) drew attention to how business and private industry managers used cultural factors to encourage change with staff. In 1990, Peter Senge's book on the "learning organization" in the corporate world found its way into educational readership. Senge and others (Block, 1993; Galagan, 1994; Whyte, 1994) emphasized the importance of nurturing individual staff members and supporting the collective engagement of staff in activities such as shared vision development, problem identification, learning, and problem resolution.

In education, Susan Rosenholtz (1989) introduced teachers' workplace factors into the literature on teaching quality. In a similar vein, Fullan (1991) recommended a "redesign of the workplace so that innovation and improvement are built into the daily activities of teachers" (p. 353). McLaughlin and Talbert (1993) confirmed Rosenholtz's findings; Darling-Hammond (1996) added to the discussion, citing shared decision making as a factor related to reform and the transformation of teaching roles in some schools. In such schools, scheduled time was provided for teachers to work together planning instruction, observing each other's classrooms, and sharing feedback.

In general, the literature describes the new workplace as an environment where structures and schedules support the gathering of all the professional staff in the school (teachers, administrators, counselors, librarians) regularly and frequently. At these times, staff members reflect on their work and assess their effectiveness in terms of benefits to their students. When areas of ineffectiveness are identified, staff members determine and plan for how they will learn new content and processes that will enable them to be more effective. Following this collective learning, staff members apply new strategies in their classrooms, evaluate their success, and make adjustments. Such continuous learning by staff results in more successful learning for students.

In these schools, collaboration is the norm. It is characterized by the staff's interdependent relationships, with all individuals engaged in a common purpose and where people rely on each other to reach agreed-upon goals that they would not be able to achieve independently.

These school staffs value change in their personal professional practice and seek changes that will improve their work and their schools. This *new approach* to improvement through a continuous emphasis on professional learning in community—learning in a social context—is adding value for the staff and students alike, as well as for the school.

—Shirley M. Hord

Acknowledgments

We recognize the opportunity given to us by the leadership at Southwest Educational Development Laboratory (SEDL) in Austin, Texas, to participate in a five-year research project titled *Creating Communities of Continuous Inquiry and Improvement*. We sincerely thank the project's research assistants and supporting staff. We also acknowledge the group of educators, called the Co-Developers, who worked diligently as external change agents in developing professional learning communities in PreK–12 schools, and the school staffs that worked to make it happen.

We are especially thankful for our research team, our contributing authors, Anita M. Pankake, D'Ette Fly Cowan, Dianne F. Olivier, and Gayle Moller. Their enduring friendships, hard work, wise counsel, and devotion to improving schools for students continue to be a source of inspiration.

We express our gratitude to our secretaries and administrative assistants, Maya Kuliga and Roger Aalderks of Cardinal Stritch University, and Robin Atteberry and Destinie Noles of the University of North Texas, for their tireless assistance on many projects throughout the evolution of this book.

We appreciate the support we have received from our deans and College of Education colleagues at the University of North Texas and Cardinal Stritch University.

Our sincere thanks to Linda Stromberg, Dallas, Texas, and Frannie Sullivan Glosson, McHenry, Illinois, who reviewed our manuscript and gave substantive content, format, and grammatical suggestions.

And, finally, we are grateful for our friends, Sharon Elkouri and Judy Colletti, for their unfailing patience, advice, and encouragement during these past three years. We end by honoring and offering our heartfelt thanks to our families—parents, siblings, and children—for the love and support they have given us throughout our lives.

Introduction

With increased external pressure for accountability in schools, teacher retention concerns, and the continuing challenge to serve diverse learners, school leaders are seeking alternative ways to address these issues. New approaches come and go, but few result in significant school improvement or student learning. If researchers are accurate in maintaining that professional learning communities (PLCs) are the "best hope" for school reform, then school leaders must be provided the knowledge and skills to create them. Many schools are integrating useful strategies, but little has been documented about their successes. In response to this perplexing situation, we reveal a comprehensive approach to document efforts toward creating PLCs.

Over a decade ago, in *Restructuring America's Schools*, Lewis (1989) asserted, "If schools are, as some charge, 'dismal places to work and learn,' it is because people have created them as such" (p. 220). School leaders and leadership preparation programs must address this issue and work to eliminate the apathy and mistrust that currently exist in some schools. The intent of this book is to highlight successful practices of emerging PLCs—inclusive, vibrant, and enduring places of learning. We capture the details of the stories of six schools in the midst of purposeful change to provide insights into their successes and struggles. Each school's journey differs because of the unique contexts, issues, and people, yet we find many of their practices similar. To illustrate the progression toward change, the stories presented are drawn from a synthesis of interview data collected across schools. We also offer case studies that present to the reader challenging issues around the development of PLCs.

BACKGROUND

In contrast to the scientific management theory of organizing schools that dominated in the early part of the twentieth century, work during the same period by James (1958) and Dewey (1938) in progressive education led to the current constructivist ideologies that link learning with experience and context. This early constructivist research is supported in the work of recent theorists (DuFour & Eaker, 1998; Hord, 1997; McLaughlin, 1993; Newmann & Wehlage, 1995; Senge, 1990), who proposed that professional learning communities, an approach to engaging school staffs in meaningful learning, can lead to increased student achievement.

In addition, during the 1980s, governmental and private sector leaders initiated efforts to address reform concerns. Response to the alarming 1983 National Commission on Excellence in Education report, *A Nation at Risk*, created a multitude of task forces collectively called "The Excellence Movement." This initiative offered an opportunity for educators to embark on serious reform of the educational system. No doubt the intentions were noble and efforts were made to improve education for students; however, there were few new systemic initiatives or creative advances. Students and teachers were told to work harder and accomplish more with fewer resources. This bureaucratic top-down approach succeeded in alienating teachers and administrators, thus widening the gap between the decision making of policymakers and the real work in the classroom.

The next two decades witnessed a proliferation of initiatives to improve schools, and ultimately, student learning. Documentation of a limited number of successful reform efforts provides evidence that *some* school efforts have resulted in increased student achievement (Hord, 1997; Louis, Kruse, & Marks, 1996). However, despite great enthusiasm and substantial work by educators, parents, and community members, advances in the majority of schools have yet to occur. In fact, problems related to discipline; parent, community, and central office support; and teacher retention and motivation continue to be barriers that inhibit schools from being successful in providing quality learning environments for students. At the same time, other issues have developed into new situational urgencies, such as the outbreak of student violence in schools and the significance of technology in the classroom.

THE CHALLENGE OF DEVELOPING PLCs

Since Peter Senge published his landmark book in 1990, *The Fifth Discipline*, both the corporate world and leading educators have been struggling with ways to foster and sustain learning organizations, cultures that provide hope for organizational reform. Kimberly Ridley, editor of *Hope Magazine*, captures the essence of this ideal: "Hope asks you to look life right in the eye—into the deep dark well of grief and wonder, fear and joy—and still see the glimmer" (2002, p. 3). For years, educators have sustained their commitment to students on merely a glimmer. Our research leaves us optimistic that, for staff to be motivated, they must believe that schools can be transformed.

Practitioners and researchers alike have provided organizations a myriad of images as to "how" these learning communities should look, but few have formed these visions into reality because little has been documented as to how to create, much less sustain, these communities of learning (Darling-Hammond, 1996; DuFour & Eaker, 1998; Fullan, 2000; Hord, 1997; Senge, 1990). In an interview with Zempke (1999), Senge described the task as formidable, "a slippery concept to put into practice" (p. 41). Thus the challenge of moving from concept to capability—initiation to implementation to institutionalization—continues (Fullan, 2000). We have found Fullan's framework simple in concept, yet complex in practice. Thus, we have chosen to use this model as the guiding structure for our book.

We now struggle to determine more relevant approaches to improve schools. Of late, researchers have embraced the concept of PLCs as the basis for essential school reform (Louis & Kruse, 1995; Mitchell & Sackney, 2001; Sergiovanni, 1992). In PLCs, teachers are involved in the school in ways that go beyond their classroom instructional roles, and leadership pervades the organization. Leaders purposefully engage faculty, staff, and administrators in building individual, interpersonal, and organizational capacity (Levy & Levy, 1993; Mitchell & Sackney, 2001).

Collaborating with Hord at the Southwest Educational Development Laboratory (SEDL), we worked as external change agents with staff, administrators, and faculty in 18 schools to model and help to facilitate the development of PLCs over a three-year period. Using a variety of methods, extensive data were collected and analyzed over the course of this project. Eventually, six schools were identified for study because they showed the most progress as they began to initiate, implement, and institutionalize—reculturing their schools into learning communities.

PURPOSE OF THE BOOK

The purpose of this book is to present *a new approach* to school improvement. We begin by documenting and examining efforts taking place in schools that are actively engaged in creating PLCs. We review evidence from site interviews to uncover exemplars and non-exemplars that validate practices promoting and practices hindering school improvement efforts. We present an assessment tool that will assist school leaders in initiating and implementing learning communities. We also document practices in case studies that will challenge readers who are interested in learning about PLCs. We hope our findings assist leaders and external change agents in guiding schools toward creating and maintaining PLCs as they move from initiation to implementation and ultimately to institutionalization (Fullan, 1985), the level necessary for sustained improvement for student learning.

ORGANIZATION OF THE BOOK

In conceptualizing this book, our research team members were eager to reveal the rich information shared with us by teachers and administrators in schools. It is our intent that readers use this information in PreK–12 schools and in leadership preparation courses. Specifically, our book provides the following:

- a report of evidence gathered from 64 interviews of faculty and staff in six PreK–12 schools during a three-year period;

- a clear picture of the progressive development of PLCs from initiation to implementation;
- a presentation of a newly developed tool to assist in the diagnosis and evaluation of PLCs;
- an analysis of the connection between school improvement and PLCs;
- an opportunity for educators to address issues facing five case study schools as they work to create PLCs; and
- reflections on our research and the generation of next steps that address the challenge of institutionalizing significant school improvement efforts to affect student learning.

Part 1, chapter 1, first provides a review of the literature surrounding PLCs in an educational context. Second, it defines and identifies the five distinguishing dimensions of a professional learning community based on Hord's research (1997). Chapter 2 reveals the methodology of the study, which includes the demographics of the study schools. We display a matrix showing the interrelationships across the five dimensions, and present a new organizational framework. The chapter also includes Fullan's (1985) change model—initiation, implementation, and institutionalization. Part 2, chapters 3 to 7, provides evidence of the progressive development of a PLC from initiation to implementation using exemplars and non-exemplars that either hinder or facilitate creating and sustaining PLCs. Part 3, chapter 8 introduces an assessment tool that enables leaders to diagnose and evaluate school efforts. Chapter 9 provides connections to school improvement using specific school examples and application of the five PLC dimensions.

Part 4, chapters 10 to 15, presents case studies related to the five dimensions of a PLC and related indicators. These real-life stories offer students in educational leadership and administration programs and other educators opportunities to engage in reflection, open dialogue, problem finding, and problem solving. Readers of these case studies are provided with an increased knowledge of a comprehensive, long-term project devoted to the creation of professional learning communities. They will gain firsthand, documented information about schools committed to change and the unique issues involving the complexity of transforming schools. Further, students will engage in problem-based learning that can transfer to their own organizations.

Part 5, chapter 16, reports lessons learned from the current study, which serves to reconceptualize Hord's view of a professional learning community. This chapter examines what it would take for schools to progress from initiation to implementation to institutionalization, including related research.

1

THE CHALLENGE OF DEVELOPING PLCs

1

Overview of Professional Learning Communities

Anita M. Pankake and Gayle Moller

In 1989 President Bush convened the governors to dialogue about the United States' education dilemma. Their work resulted in the creation of *Goals 2000*, a list of objectives that students and schools should aspire to by the end of the century. Congress added two additional goals to make the total eight. These goals included: 1) getting students ready to learn; 2) increasing graduation rates; 3) expanding student competency in crucial subject areas; 4) increasing emphasis in math and science; 5) increasing adult literacy; 6) decreasing drugs and violence on campuses; 7) providing opportunities for professional development; and 8) boosting parental involvement. Reaction to *Goals 2000* fostered the emergence of the Restructuring Movement, which took many different forms. Central to these reforms was the management of schools at the site level, not the district level. The hope was that administrators and teachers could collaboratively make decisions to develop policies, procedures, and strategies that would realistically and effectively address the needs of schools and students (Lieberman, 1995).

WHY DEVELOP PROFESSIONAL LEARNING COMMUNITIES?

The No Child Left Behind Act of 2001 is the most sweeping reform of the Elementary and Secondary Education Act (ESEA) since ESEA was enacted in 1965. Consequently, policymakers are demanding specific, challenging

3

outcomes that will be difficult to realize even for schools that previously made satisfactory progress based on the average of their students' achievement. Students with special needs who previously were not tested will be assessed under this law. Walker (2002) stated, "In a high-stakes context, school leaders must search for ways to create a culture of high expectations and support for all students and set of norms around teacher growth that enables teachers to teach all students well" (p. 3).

In response to these external pressures, school-based reform has been widespread and varied in form. Efforts differ in duration, amount of collaboration, position levels invited to participate, and professional development focus. Shields and Knapp (1997) noted that school-based reform is not a guarantee for increased student learning. Their work revealed that reforms with the most promise share five common characteristics: a) a set of attainable reform goals with long time lines for accomplishing them; b) a focus explicitly on particular aspects of the curriculum and instructional practices while aligning professional development with these changes; c) putting in place a school-level process for considering changes in practice while refraining from making school governance the main preoccupation of the reform effort; d) encouraging collaborative engagement of staff members with one another; and e) using professional development resources to further this end. The established professional learning community is a reform initiative that reflects these characteristics.

School reforms often fail due to the lack of attention paid to building a school culture that supports teacher development through collaborative adult learning. Professional learning communities are not only a school-based reform; their establishment also creates a structure helpful for sustaining other initiatives intended to foster school improvement. Consequently, professional learning communities are increasingly identified as critical to the success of school reform efforts (Bryk, Easton, Rollow, & Sebring, 1994; Louis, Kruse, & Marks, 1996; McLaughlin, 1993; Newmann & Wehlage, 1995). A professional learning community is defined as a school's professional staff members who continuously seek to find answers through inquiry and act on their learning to improve student learning (Astuto, Clark, Read, McGree, & Fernandez, 1993). As noted by Newmann (1999), "Change in education comes about only when teachers are helped to change themselves" (p. 294).

This reculturing of schools has been characterized by shared values and norms, an emphasis on student learning, reflective dialogue, deprivatization of practice, and collaboration (Louis et al., 1996). Sergiovanni (1994) called on schools to become communities where professional learning is continuous, reflective, and focused on improving student outcomes. But building a professional learning community is difficult due to the many demands on teachers and administrators; the growing accountability issues; the increasingly diverse needs of students; teacher isolation and burnout; and many other unmanageable stressors. To develop, nurture, and sustain a community of learners means creating a different culture that includes a shared vision, true collaboration, administrator and teacher leadership, and conditions that support these efforts (Mitchell & Sackney, 2000). According to DuFour and Eaker, "There is growing evidence that the best hope for significant school improvement is transforming schools into professional learning communities" (1998, p. 17). The challenge that this statement describes invites educators to examine the guiding principles of professional learning communities to determine what we must do for substantive school improvement. Newmann and Wehlage (1995) described professional community as schools "characterized by shared purpose, collaborative activity, and collective responsibility among staff" (p. 37).

The term "professional learning community" also emerged from organizational theory and human relations literature. Senge (1990) defined a learning organization as one in which "people continually expand their capacity to create desired results, where new and expansive patterns of thinking are nurtured, where collective aspiration is set free" (p. 3). In an interview with Sparks (1999), Lieberman described professional learning communities as "places in which teachers pursue clear, shared purposes for student learning, engage in collaborative activities to achieve their purposes, and take collective responsibility for student learning" (p. 53).

DIMENSIONS OF A
PROFESSIONAL LEARNING COMMUNITY

Hord (1997a) defined professional learning community as the professional staff learning together to direct efforts toward improved student learning. Her work reflects the work of several researchers (Kleine-Kracht, 1993; Leithwood, Leonard, & Sharratt, 1997; Louis & Kruse, 1995; Sergiovanni, 1994; Snyder, Acker-Hocevar, & Snyder, 1996). She identified five dimensions characteristic of schools with successful professional learning communities in place. These dimensions are used to organize this review of literature. Hord's five dimensions are listed in figure 1.1.

Supportive and Shared Leadership

Hord (1997) explained that supportive and shared leadership are applied when school administrators participate democratically with teachers sharing power, authority, and decision making. It is clear that effective school communities have shared leadership extending throughout the school to faculty, staff, and administrators. Eaker, DuFour, and Burnette (2002) characterized the new view of school leadership:

---

1. *Supportive and shared leadership*: School administrators participate democratically with teachers by sharing power, authority, and decision making, and by promoting and nurturing leadership among staff.
2. *Shared values and vision*: Staff shares visions for school improvement that have an undeviating focus on student learning. Shared values support norms of behavior that guide decisions about teaching and learning.
3. *Collective learning and application*: Staff at all levels of the school shares information and works collaboratively to plan, solve problems, and improve learning opportunities. Together they seek knowledge, skills, and strategies and apply this new learning to their work.
4. *Supportive conditions*: Collegial relationships include respect, trust, norms of critical inquiry and improvement, and positive, caring relationships among students, teachers, and administrators. Structures include a variety of conditions such as size of the school, proximity of staff to one another, communication systems, and the time and space for staff to meet and examine current practices.
5. *Shared personal practice*: Peers visit with and observe one another to offer encouragement and to provide feedback on instructional practices to assist in student achievement and increase individual and organizational capacity.

Source: Hipp, K. A., & Huffman, J. B. (2002). *Documenting and examining practices in creating learning communities: Exemplars and non-exemplars*, modified from Hord, S. M. (1997a). *Professional learning communities: Communities of continuous inquiry and improvement*. Austin, TX: Southwest Educational Development Laboratory.

Figure 1.1. Dimensions of professional learning communities.

One of the most fundamental cultural shifts that takes place as schools become professional learning communities involves how teachers are viewed. In traditional schools, administrators are viewed as being in leadership positions, while teachers are viewed as "implementors" or followers. In professional learning communities, administrators are viewed as leaders of leaders. (p. 22)

Successful communities of learners share important concerns and relationships in their efforts to achieve results for students. This requires a new concept of leadership in which administrators and teachers take responsibility for leadership and decision making. Glickman (2002) suggested that if a school leader understands that the "use of multiple structures with multiple leaders for assisting, focusing, and improving classroom teaching and learning, then continuous improvement can become an ongoing reality" (p. 9). In her landmark book, *Leading to Change*, Johnson (1996) emphasized,

> Today's school leaders must understand both the limits and the potential of their positions, carefully balancing their use of positional authority with their reliance on others, gradually building both a capacity and widespread support for shared leadership and collaborative change. (p. 11)

Furthermore, shared leadership promotes a multitude of interactions and relationships that build capacity for change. Fullan (2002) asserted, "The role of leadership is to 'cause' greater capacity in the organization in order to get better results" (p. 65).

Shared Values and Vision

It becomes readily apparent in school organizations that if you don't have a vision, it is impossible to develop effective policies, procedures, and strategies targeted toward a future goal and aligned to provide consistent implementation of programs. Senge (1990) stated, "You cannot have a learning organization without a shared vision" (p. 209). An effective vision presents a credible yet realistic picture of the organization that inspires the participants to reach for a future goal. According to Hord (1997b), the concept of a learning community embraces shared values and vision that "lead to binding norms of behavior that the staff supports" (p. 3). This vision for school improvement emerges when it is characterized by an undeviating focus on student learning.

Yet simply declaring a vision by a school leader and imposing it on the organization will not generate the collective energy needed to propel an organization forward. The central task of the leader is to involve others in creating a shared vision for the organization. Personal visions must be developed and shared so that a collective vision can be molded and embraced by all members. This collaborative vision building is the initial challenge for learning communities. DuFour and Eaker (1998) addressed shared vision as follows:

> What separates a learning community from an ordinary school is its collective commitment to guiding principles that articulate what the people in the school believe and what they seek to create. Furthermore, these guiding principles are not just articulated by those in positions of leadership; even more important, they are embedded in the hearts and minds of people throughout the school. (p. 25)

Developing this capacity to construct meaning represented by a vision is a formidable task. It is a task that many schools do not even begin to address. Barth (1990a) suggested one way to begin designing this shared vision:

> Honoring the visions of others, maintaining fidelity to one's own vision, and at the same time working toward a collective vision and coherent institutional purpose constitute an extraordinary definition of school leadership and represent one of the most important undertakings facing those who would improve schools from within. (p. 156)

The creation of a school vision, as an integral component of the change process, emerges over time and is based on common values and beliefs. DuFour and Eaker (1998) examined the co-creation of a shared vision and suggested,

> The lack of a compelling vision for public schools continues to be a major obstacle in any effort to improve schools. Until educators can describe the school they are trying to create, it is impossible to develop policies, procedures, or programs that will help make that ideal a reality. . . . Building a

shared vision is the ongoing, never-ending, daily challenge confronting all who hope to create learning communities. (p. 64)

Understanding this challenge reinforces the fact that developing a shared vision based on common values varies as widely as the schools themselves. Each school is unique. Fullan and Miles argued, "There can be no blueprints for change that transfer from one school to the next" (cited in Brown, 1995, p. 92).

Little (1997) explained the individuality of each school by suggesting that values are embedded in the day-to-day actions of the school staff resulting in norms that honor and develop the commitment and talents of individuals seeking to improve their learning communities. The process of defining values and determining which ones to include in teaching and learning presents confusing issues. Begley and Johannson (2000) referred to the often-quoted definition of values by Kluckhohn: "Values are a conception, explicit or implicit, distinctive of an individual or characteristic of a group, of the desirable which influences the selection from available modes, means, and ends of action" (pp. 5–6).

Knowing that values are essential for school communities is only a beginning. There must also be an organized or structured mechanism to identify the desired values and teach them. Developing a vision statement is one way to achieve the inclusion of values in the school culture.

Unfortunately, school reform efforts have been generally unsuccessful in providing the leadership, understanding, and motivation needed to empower staff to create the collective vision based on shared values that align curriculum, instruction, assessment, and supporting programs for schools (Fullan, 1995; Guskey & Peterson, 1993; Lindle, 1995/1996; Newmann & Wehlage, 1995). Some research suggests that developing professional learning communities might be the organizational strategy that could make school reform more successful (DuFour & Eaker, 1998; Louis & Kruse, 1995).

Collective Learning and Application

Collective learning and application refers to the "staff's collective learning and application of the learnings (taking action) that create high intellectual tasks and solutions to address student needs" (Hord, 1997).

Mention the words "staff development" and most teachers envision a workshop, a conference, or some other source of external expertise (Moore & Shaw, 2000). This form of traditional staff development is still prevalent in most schools and school systems. Even though there is a consensus about what constitutes effective professional development, traditional models continue to prevail (Hawley & Valli, 1999; National Staff Development Council, 2001). Fortunately there are schools where collective learning is the norm (Stein, 1998), but there are relatively few models, and these schools are precariously held together by a dependency on the leadership in the principal's office (Davidson & Dell, 1996; Silins, Mulford, & Zarins, 1999).

A new approach for professional development is needed to help teachers recognize the value of their own craft knowledge and of learning with others within their schools (Dunne & Honts, 1998; Moore & Shaw, 2000). Teachers within professional learning communities share their practices, study together, focus instructional strategies on student needs, and use data to make decisions about their teaching.

Learning that takes place within the school becomes job-embedded where there is a just-in-time need for information (Wood & Killian, 1998). Job-embedded learning involves "learning by doing, reflecting on the experience, and then generating and sharing new insights and learning with oneself and others" (Wood & McQuarrie, 1999, p. 10). Workshops and other traditional staff development, conducted by external "experts" are not eliminated from the menu of options for teacher learning, but these are selected through strategic decisions to enrich the collective learning within the school. Professional development then becomes an ongoing activity that is embedded in the various educational processes of operating schools—curriculum development, student assessment, and the development and evaluation of instructional strategies. Because it is embedded, professional development becomes "an indispensable part of all forms of leadership and collegial sharing" (Guskey, 2000, p. 38).

An outcome of collective learning within a professional learning community is the emergence of teacher leadership. Once teachers witness the benefits of learning with others in the school, they recognize the need to share in the leadership to develop a shared vision focused on student learning (Foster & Suddards, 1999). Teachers recognize that engaging in such collaboration "*implies* opportunity *and* obligation" (Stein, 1998, p. 8).

Rather than depending on external measures of accountability, perhaps teachers can take on the responsibility for documenting their students' learning.

Defining teacher leadership helps to clarify the difference between those teachers who want to remain close to the classroom and those who seek administrative positions or formal roles. Teachers who are leaders lead within and beyond the classroom, contribute to a community of leaders and learners, and influence others toward improved educational practice (Katzenmeyer & Moller, 2001). Such leadership can be viewed as "a set of functions rather than a formal role" (Lieberman 1992, p. 163). Schools and school districts may invite teachers to take on formal roles within their schools, but many teacher leaders take on tasks that appeal to their passion without seeking positional power. These teachers influence their colleagues toward improved practice by being perceived as competent, credible, and approachable (Katzenmeyer & Moller, 2001).

The potential for positive benefits from teacher leadership in school restructuring and reform has led to a proliferation of research on the concept, leadership roles teachers can assume, and school cultures that encourage and support teacher leadership (Lambert, 1998; Lieberman, Falk, & Alexander, 1995). Benefits of teacher leadership include improved teaching and learning (Ovando, 1994); teacher efficacy (Hipp, 1997; Short, 1994); retention of excellent teachers (Gordon, 1991; Hart & Murphy, 1990); commitment to change efforts (Firestone, 1996; Rosenholtz, 1989); enhanced teacher careers (Fullan, 2001); and increased teacher accountability for results (Darling-Hammond, 1990).

Shared Personal Practice

Midgley and Wood (1993) contended that "teachers need an environment that values and supports hard work, the acceptance of challenging tasks, risk taking, and the promotion of growth" (p. 252). An environment that values such endeavors is enhanced by processes that encourage teachers to share their personal practices with one another. According to Hord (1997a), this dimension necessitates peer review and feedback on instructional practice in order to increase individual and organizational capacity.

Louis and Kruse (1995) called this "deprivatization of practice" and maintained that review of a teacher's instructional practice by colleagues is the norm in the professional learning community. This review is not an evaluative procedure, but serves as a part of the "peers helping peers" process. One example of this practice is for teachers to present student work (products) to colleagues to be reviewed as evidence of quality instructional practice. Another example is for teachers to visit their colleagues' classrooms in order to observe, script notes, and discuss their observations. Within professional learning communities, these types of activities are highly valued and occur on a regular, ongoing basis with a structured process to guide the interaction.

Underlying this process is the desire for both individual and whole-school improvement, and it is rendered possible only after mutual respect and trustworthiness has been established among staff members. Wignall (1992) described a high school in which teachers share their practice and enjoy high levels of collaboration in their daily work life. He noted that mutual respect and understanding are fundamental requirements of this kind of workplace culture . This culture fosters an environment in which teachers find help from, support, and trust their colleagues as a result of the development of warm, professional relationships. Teachers participate in debate, discussion, and disagreement; they share their successes and their failures. But they are always collectively committed to the work of increasing student learning.

Supportive Conditions

Supporting the work of learning communities requires leaders to address the fifth dimension: supportive conditions. Hord (1997a) defined this dimension as school conditions and capacities that support the staff's arrangement as a professional learning organization. Researchers (Boyd, 1992; DuFour & Eaker, 1998; Louis & Kruse, 1995) noted two types of conditions as necessary to build effective learning communities: the people capacities of those involved and the physical, or structural, conditions. These factors support the work of teachers and administrators by providing time and opportunities to communicate regularly, plan collectively, problem solve, and learn.

Louis and Kruse (1995) identified physical conditions needed to support communities of learners to include time to meet and dialogue; physical proximity of the staff to one another in departments or grade level groups; small school size; collaborative teaching roles and responsibilities; effective communication programs; autonomous school units that are connected in meaningful ways to the district office and personnel; and teacher leadership that provides opportunities for teachers to influence decision making.

These structural conditions are clearly important so staff and administration have available resources to conduct their work without major logistical barriers. However, Schlechty (1997) pointed out that "structural change that is not supported by cultural change will eventually be overwhelmed by the culture, for it is in the culture that any organization finds meaning and stability" (p. 136).

Boyd (1992) described the people or cultural factors that create a meaningful and stable culture. Such factors include teacher attitudes that are consistently positive; an academic focus for students; norms that support ongoing learning and improvement, not the status quo; a collective shared vision; participatory decision making; teachers who share and learn with each other; and a sense of responsibility for student learning and success.

Time for teachers to work together is the factor described as critical for supporting school reform initiatives (Hoerr, 1996). Common planning time within the regular workday provides teachers the professional time necessary for collaborative work without impinging on their personal time (Zinn, 1997). National reports on the use of time in schools proliferated during the middle 1990s (National Education Association Special Committee on Time Resources, 1993; National Education Commission on Time and Learning, 1994; Purnell & Hill, 1992). These reports pointed out that time in the school day must be restructured to provide educators time to make meaning of the new changes demanded of them. Since these reports were released, relatively little energy has been spent on the time issue except for journal articles that deal with strategies to work within the existing structure. The authors of the National Commission for Teaching and America's Future (1996) directed attention to the root cause of the time issue when they revealed that the United States did not focus its resources on the classroom, but put valuable funds into personnel outside the classroom.

Principal leadership continues to be proclaimed as the key factor in the success of professional learning communities (Larsen & Malen, 1997; Spaulding, 1994). In the present leadership structure of most schools, the principal is the person who is responsible for providing supportive conditions for the professional learning community. Distribution of resources, both fiscal and human, is the responsibility of the principal as mandated by school district policies and state laws. In spite of rather inflexible structures, many principals are breaking from the norm and engaging other members of the school community in decision making (Svec, Pourdavood, & Cowen, 1999). The ability of principals to relinquish power is essential for the support of professional learning communities. Also, as co-learner, the principal models the level of learning expected from the professional staff.

SUMMARY

The literature base related to professional learning communities becomes richer each year; the advocates for this reculturing effort have increased in number among both practitioners and researchers. The dearth is in information on how this reculturing occurs.

The next chapter of this book helps to fill the void of "how" professional learning communities are formed. Chapter 2 also offers information regarding the methods used to gather and analyze data during three phases of research over a three-year period. The description sets the framework for presenting findings from this research that help bring greater detail to the picture of how professional learning communities develop.

2

Responding to the Challenge

Research suggests that "change will require a radical reculturing of the school as an institution, and the basic redesign of the teaching profession" (Fullan, 1995, p. 230). Reculturing occurs by developing values, norms, and attitudes that affect the core of the culture of schools, which drives structural change. In order to reculture, there is also a need to develop capacity through distributed leadership, which necessitates shared responsibility, broad-based decision making, and more accountability across the entire school community. Our research documents beginning steps in six high-performing schools that have systematically moved through initiation and implementation to reculture their current organizations. The next section in this chapter familiarizes the reader with a brief description of the phases of our research study.

METHODOLOGY

The research that undergirds the findings in this book is the final component of a multi-method, five-year study (1995–2000) of the development of professional learning communities (PLCs)—schools that continuously inquire and seek to improve teaching and learning (see figure 2.1).

In *Phase 1* (1995–1996) Shirley M. Hord, senior research associate at the Southwest Educational Development Laboratory (SEDL), conducted an extensive review of the literature surrounding PLCs related to schools,

1995–1996—Phase 1	• Review of the literature
1996–1997	• Search for PLC schools
1997–1998—Phase 2	• Training of Co-Developers • Selection of study sites • *School Professional Staff as Learning Community Questionnaire*
1998–1999	• Continuous training of Co-Developers • Initial phone interviews with school principals and teacher representatives • *School Professional Staff as Learning Community Questionnaire*
1999–2000—Phase 3	• Continuous training of Co-Developers • Follow-up interviews with school principals and teacher representatives • On-site interviews of teaching staff in study schools conducted by SEDL staff and Co-Developer • *School Professional Staff as Learning Community Questionnaire*

Figure 2.1.   Five-year PLC project.

businesses, and other organizations. As a result of this review, Hord conceptualized five dimensions that reflect the essence of a PLC: shared and supportive leadership; shared vision and values; collective learning and application; supportive conditions (relationships and structures); and shared personal practice. During 1996–1997, the SEDL staff searched for schools in its five-state region that characterized the above dimensions. Hord found, as others have, that these schools were rare.

In *Phase 2* (1997–1998), Hord—as manager of the Creating Communities of Continuous Inquiry and Improvement project, a federally funded project to create PLCs—invited 30 educators from around the nation to participate in this venture. During this phase, our role as project Co-Developers, or external change agents, was to understand the challenge of this undertaking. We shared expertise, developed plans, and created materials that might promote our success in creating PLCs in a variety of PreK–12 contexts. We collected and analyzed data from our study sites, which included phone interviews (Fall–Spring, 1998–1999), face-to-face interviews with principals and lead teachers from each of the original study sites (Summer, 1999), and the administration of Hord's (1998) PLC questionnaire, *School Professional Staff as Learning Community*. The questionnaire, which was constructed around Hord's five dimensions, was administered three consecutive years to the entire faculty at each school site. Individuals who wish to preview the instrument should contact the Southwest Educational Development ment Laboratory (SEDL), 1-800-476-6861, and speak to the communications specialist, or e-mail Shirley M. Hord at shord@sedl.org.

By *Phase 3* of the project, only 12 schools remained. During the 1999–2000 school year, the final data for this project, which included 106 on-site, structured interviews, were collected and analyzed. Our intent was to hear from a representative sample, beyond the principal and lead teacher (who were most committed to the PLC project), and to gain further insight into the implementation. The results from this representative sample produced six schools that exhibited characteristics of many dimensions of a PLC. It is from these schools that we draw exemplars and non-exemplars.

The six high-readiness schools were located primarily in the South and Midwest regions of the nation. In their efforts to create PLCs, all schools included in this sample had progressed from the level of initiation to implementation. The schools included elementary, middle, and high school grade levels, as well as a diverse population of students in rural, suburban and urban settings. These schools included students who were economically disadvantaged (qualified for free and reduced lunch) to varying degrees (see table 2.1).

The 64 interviews from the six study schools (see figure 2.2 for interview protocol) were conducted on-site and lasted 30–60 minutes. They

Table 2.1.   High readiness schools demographics. Courtesy Shirley Hord, 1998.

Name of School	Level	Grade Levels	Context	Number of Students	Economically Disadvantaged	Number of Interviews
Davis	Primary	PreK–3	Rural	196	63%	12
Lakeland	Elementary	PreK–8	Urban	960	27%	7
Foxdale	Middle School	5–8	Suburban	550	12%	13
Northland	Elementary	K–5	Suburban	537	59%	16
Glen Rock	High School	9–12	Rural	410	22%	7
Kennedy	Middle School	6–8	Suburban	971	87%	9

Supportive & Shared Leadership:
Our intent is to find out what they think leadership is and if and how widely leadership is shared among administrators and teachers. Ask for evidence that supports their comments.

Tell me about leadership in this school.

Use these probes:
- Who are the leaders?
- What do they do that makes them leaders?
- Is leadership shared? If so, how?
- Tell me how decisions get made. About what? By whom? Etc.
- How did this decision-making process come about? By whom?
- Give an example of how a school decision was made recently.

Is this different from the past? If so, who or what has made it different?

Shared Values & Vision:
Our intent is to find out the values behind the vision, who was involved in creating the vision, and who believes in it. Ask for evidence that supports their comments.

Tell me what the staff would say is important about the work they do here.

Use these probes:
- How do you know?
- How is it reflected in the school?
- In the classroom?
- With students?

Tell me about the school's vision of improvement.

Use these probes:
- What process did the school use to create a vision?
- Who decided on this vision? How does the staff feel about it?
- How is the vision communicated? Externally? Internally?
- How is the vision reflected in the school activities and operation?

Is this different from the past? If so, who or what has made it different?

Collective Learning & Application:
Our intent is to find out if all of the staff members come together to reflect on their work for students and learn from each other in substantive dialogue. Ask for evidence that supports their comments.

Tell me about how the staff comes together to learn.

Use these probes:
- How many of the staff come together to learn?
- When? How often? About what?
- How do staff members determine what they want to learn?
- Tell me about how the staff uses what they learn.

Is this different from the past? If so, who or what has made it different?

Figure 2.2.   Communities of continuous inquiry and improvement research protocol.

Supportive Conditions:
Our intent is to find out what is in place—**structures** (for example, time and space for staff to meet) and **relationships** the staff has with each other that support teachers' work together. Ask for evidence that supports their comments.

Tell me about conditions in the school that support teachers' work together.
Use these probes:
- What structures support collective learning?
- How do staff members communicate with each other?
- How do they communicate with people outside of the school?
- When do teachers have time to collaborate?
- What resources are available to support teachers learning together?
- How do staff members work with each other? Cooperate? Support?
- Who are the staff members that motivate and inspire?

Is this different from the past? If so, who or what has made it different?

Shared Personal Practice (Peers Sharing with Peers):
Our intent is to find out if the staff is sharing their work with each other and then giving relevant feedback that will improve teacher practice—ask for evidence that supports their comments.

Tell me about any situations in which the staff shares their practice and solicits feedback from each other to improve their teaching (e.g., classroom observation, examining student work).
Use these probes:
- Do teachers go into each other's classrooms to observe them at work with students?
- Do teachers work together to examine student work?
- Do they give substantive feedback to each other on their observations or on student work?
- How do you know what to look for in giving peer review and feedback?
- How did these processes come about? Who initiates them?
- How are they integrated into the school schedule?

Is this different from the past? If so, who or what has made it different?

Figure 2.2. (*Continued*)

were tape-recorded, transcribed, and analyzed using Hord's five dimensions. Although these dimensions may appear preconceived and suggest a deterministic approach, this system of data collection and analysis seemed rational since the six high-readiness schools were intentional in their efforts to apply these dimensions to initiate and work toward the development of a PLC. Moreover, researchers analyzed interviews using a variety of related indicators to examine and substantiate the thoroughness of Hord's five-dimensional model. Using qualitative analysis methods, we identified themes evolving from initiation to implementation that serve as the critical attributes of each dimension (see figure 2.3).

Although the dimensions are separate and discreet, we analyzed them holistically due to the overlapping characteristics found within the dimensions. Morrissey (2000), a member of the SEDL staff, provides a matrix that depicts interrelationships across the dimensions (see table 2.2). Descriptors of each dimension are listed on the horizontal rows. The

---

- **Shared and Supportive Leadership**
- Nurturing leadership among staff
- Shared power, authority, and responsibility
- Broad-based decision making that reflects commitment and accountability

- **Shared Values and Vision**
- Espoused values and norms
- Focus on student learning
- High expectations
- Shared vision guides teaching and learning

- **Collective Learning and Application**
- Sharing information
- Seeking new knowledge, skills, and strategies
- Working collaboratively to plan, solve problems, and improve learning opportunities

- **Shared Personal Practice**
- Peer observations to offer knowledge, skills, and encouragement
- Feedback to improve instructional practices
- Sharing outcomes of instructional practices
- Coaching and mentoring

- **Supportive Conditions**
- Relationships
  - o Caring relationships
  - o Trust and respect
  - o Recognition and celebration
  - o Risk-taking
  - o Unified effort to embed change
- Structures
  - o Resources (time, money, materials, people)
  - o Facilities
  - o Communication systems

Figure 2.3.   PLC dimensions and critical attributes.

Table 2.2. Morrissey matrix.

Dimensions	Shared and Supportive Leadership	Shared Values and Vision	Collective Learning and Application of Learning	Supportive Conditions	Shared Personal Practice
Shared and Supportive Leadership	School administrators participate democratically with teachers, sharing power, authority, and decision making.	Together, the principal and staff decide on the values and vision of the school and support their realization.	The principal and teachers create the context in which they can focus their learning and support its implementation.	Together, the principal and teachers access resources, develop structures, and nurture relationships that support a professional learning community.	Together, the principal and staff develop ways to share practices to increase individual and organizational capacity.
Shared Values and Vision	The shared values and vision guide the principal and staff in making individual and collective decisions on substantive issues.	Staff shares visions for school improvement that have an undeviating focus on improving student learning and are consistently referenced for the staff's work.	The staff values coming together to learn ways to improve student learning consistent with the vision.	Shared values and vision guide the staff in developing physical and organizational structures and relationships that support the professional learning community.	The staff values the process of peer review and feedback to improve classroom practice consistent with the vision.
Collective Learning and Application of Learning	All staff use their learning to inform decisions and develop actions on substantive issues.	Together, all staff engage in learning that reflects their values and contributes to realizing the vision of the school.	The staff's collective learning and application of the learning (taking action) create high intellectual learning tasks and solutions to address student needs.	The staff's collective learning guides the staff in identifying and developing organizational structures and relationships that support the professional learning community.	The staff's collective learning provides a purpose and focus for peer review and feedback to improve classroom practice.

Table 2.2. (Continued)

Dimensions	Shared and Supportive Leadership	Shared Values and Vision	Collective Learning and Application of Learning	Supportive Conditions	Shared Personal Practice
Supportive Conditions	Structural conditions and collegial relationships enable the staff to participate democratically in making decisions about substantive issues.	Structural conditions and collegial relationships reinforce the staff's undeviating focus on student learning.	Structural conditions and collegial relationships provide opportunities for all staff to learn ways to improve their collective practice.	Structural conditions and collegial relationships support the staff's arrangement as a professional learning organization.	Structures and collegial relationships enable the staff to review each other's classroom practice and give feedback to improve student learning.
Shared Personal Practice	Peer review and feedback on instructional practices increase individual and organizational capacity for whole-school decision making.	Peer review and feedback on instructional practices reinforce the school's shared values and vision in the classroom.	Learning emerging from peer review and feedback informs the staff on areas for collective study to improve classroom practice.	Peer review and feedback strengthen collegial relationships and reinforce the use of organizational structures needed for sharing practice.	Peers review and give feedback on instructional practice in order to increase individual and organizational capacity.

reader can determine how one dimension influences the other four dimensions by looking down the vertical columns. For instance, in the shared and supportive leadership row in table 2.2, one can look at the values and vision column to see how leadership and values and vision merge. The value of the matrix is to illustrate the strength in the relationships among the dimensions as administrators and teachers reach beyond the traditional structures of schools toward new ways of increasing student learning.

INITIATION—IMPLEMENTATION—INSTITUTIONALIZATION

The success of any innovation and change in schools is dependent on how well staff members can sustain their efforts and embed them into the culture of their school. If new approaches are viewed as short-term, quick fixes to perceived problems, the impact will be superficial, confined to a few participants, and generally ineffective. Thus the question remains, How do schools maintain momentum and long-term success in the change process? Fullan (1990) identified 14 key success factors within three phases of change: initiation, implementation, and institutionalization (see table 2.3).

Schools in the *initiation phase* generally connect a change initiative to student needs based on the school's values and norms. A strong leader advocates the shared vision and staff begin to dialogue, share information, seek new knowledge, and commit to the effort to achieve their goals. During the *implementation phase*, the principal encourages the staff to set high expectations and enables them to meet their goals by sharing power, authority, and responsibility. Feedback and support related to instruction are evident, which leads to increased student outcomes. Nonetheless,

Table 2.3. Fullan's phases of change.

Initiation	Implementation	Institutionalization
Linked to high profile needs	Orchestration	Embedding
	Shared control	Linked to instruction
A clear model	Pressure and support	Widespread use
Strong advocate	Technical assistance	Removal of competing priorities
Active initiation	Rewards	Continuing assistance

progress is not always smooth. The initiative being implemented often mirrors Fullan's "Implementation Dip," which is a series of setbacks that often hinder progress. These setbacks are often due to a lack of resources and technical assistance and cause frustration, anxiety, and a sense of hopelessness. Staffs that prevail through these uncertain times usually move to the *institutionalization phase*, where the change initiative becomes embedded into the culture of the school. Guided by a shared vision, the school community is committed and accountable for student learning. They do so by identifying and solving problems amid a climate that invites risk and therefore continual refocusing. Institutionalization is the phase of change that has not been addressed by the vast majority of schools in their improvement efforts. This omission is reported in our research as well. Our belief is that institutionalization across the five PLC dimensions is essential for schools to engage in sustained improvement and for continuous learning to occur.

A NEW APPROACH TO CREATING PLCS

In the next five chapters we report exemplars and non-exemplars that promote or hinder school efforts under each of the five dimensions of a PLC. The current data from 64 interviews across six schools have been drawn from school principals and a purposeful sample of staff reflecting diversity in gender, subject area, and grade level. These interviews finalized a three-year period as schools moved deeper into creating a culture reflecting a PLC. Each dimension is used as an organizer to report the interview data and the progression from initiation to implementation that reflects the growth in schools seeking to become PLCs. Additionally, data are organized around our findings—the critical attributes linked to each dimension.

As we examined this final set of interviews, we conceptualized Hord's five dimensions in a new light, as illustrated in the Professional Learning Community Organizer (PLCO) (see figure 2.4). First, we saw a critical link between *collective learning and application* and *shared personal practice.* We believe that these elements could not be separated and, therefore, should be placed together in this "nonsequential" set of dimensions. Second, as the critical attributes emerged throughout these interviews, they logically fell on a continuum reflecting evidence at the levels of ini-

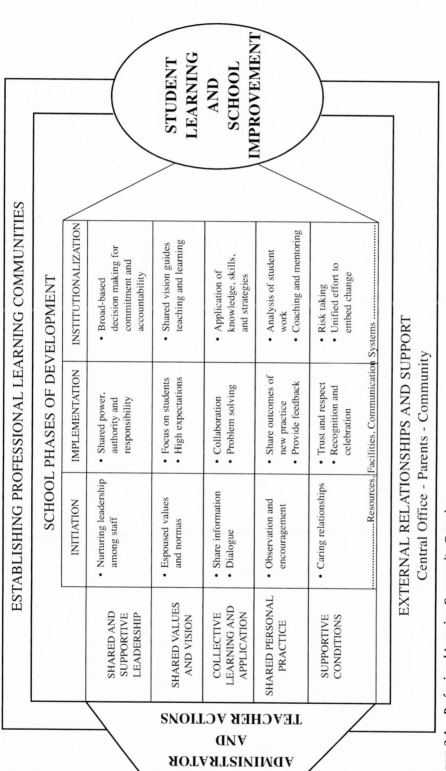

Figure 2.4.   Professional Learning Community Organizer.

tiation, implementation, and institutionalization. Third, we viewed *supportive conditions* encompassing all four dimensions, similar to the way Peter Senge views the fifth discipline of *systems thinking* (Senge, 1990). We contend that without a climate of trust and respect, and structures that promote continual learning, it is impossible to build a professional learning community.

Chapters 3–7 capture the views of teachers and principals in urban, suburban, and rural schools. Although the contexts in these schools are markedly different, we found the evidence could often be generalized across settings. Practitioners can read these descriptions and examples of the practice of other educators and see themselves in similar situations. We hope the information provided will assist administrators and teachers to find ways to adapt these real-life examples to improve their schools, increase teacher and student learning opportunities, and build the foundation for institutionalizing reform efforts.

2

FROM INITIATION TO IMPLEMENTATION: DIMENSIONS OF A PLC

Chapters 3–7 provide exemplars and non-exemplars from teacher and principal interviews that portray the progression of professional learning communities in six high-readiness schools through Fullan's (1985) phases of initiation, implementation, and institutionalization. Quotations have been carefully selected and integrated across schools and placed in an order that reflects these progressive phases as illustrated in the Professional Learning Community Organizer (PLCO) (figure 2.4).

3

Shared and Supportive Leadership

Ultimately, your leadership in a culture of change will be judged as effective or ineffective, not by who you are as a leader but by *what leadership you produce in others*.

—Michael Fullan, *Leadership in a Culture of Change*

School administrators participate democratically with teachers by sharing power, authority, and decision making, and by promoting and nurturing leadership among staff.

NURTURING LEADERSHIP AMONG STAFF

Teacher interviews indicated that principals and other administrators deliberately engaged in promoting leadership among staff; however, in some cases leadership was shared out of necessity. As one teacher remarked, "There was so much change. We restructured the whole district, got a new principal, got a new grade level in the building, and reconfigured our fifth-through eighth-grade teams. No one principal could do it all." In an elementary school, teachers viewed leadership as changing and revealed a high level of resentment and a lack of trust in years past. One teacher admitted, "When the Leadership Team came on, he [the principal] tried to hand over some leadership to us in instructional areas. We've come a long way in terms of working supportively toward change in how we teach and viewing ourselves as leaders." Teachers have stepped forward, shedding the fear of hearing their own voices: "I don't feel at all threatened to voice my opinion or my thoughts and ideas, even when they differ from the rest." Another came to realize, "We need to share our voices to be leaders. It encourages us to help each other out and work together. There's not really one person who's more important than the rest."

Teachers were also aware of being "on the other side" as leaders. One teacher admitted that, when the Leadership Team meets, they decide what will be presented and how the meeting will be structured. "We've tried to do different things in the small groups, so that they leave feeling like it wasn't a waste of time. We don't want to waste anybody's time because they will tell you quickly." Leadership Teams in schools consisted of a wide range of personalities and perspectives regardless of level. "Everybody has their niche and I think that the most change is to see kindergarten teachers working as leaders with eighth-grade physical education people to solve problems." In this school, "teachers teach teachers, like we have our computer liaison and our building computer person who train here on campus and we have the other elementary schools that come here for the training from our teachers."

Classroom teachers were most often hailed for their modeling and inspiration. "Our teachers are great at what they do. Others see this and say, 'What are you doing and I'd like to try that!'" One teacher asserted,

> The teachers here or staff members who I think are the most inspirational are those who are visionary. They know what they want and they will do anything to make it happen. Like when Julie has a vision, I get so pumped up just hearing her talk about it. I think, Yeah! Other teachers assume responsibility for work in the greater school community and lead faculty meetings, while still others lead book studies and work with the principal in how to best present it to the entire faculty.

Leadership is also promoted in teams where "there's always someone that comes forth from that grade that we can listen to." One teacher noted the efforts of the administration and maintained, "They encourage leadership. They pick a pretty good staff to begin with—teachers who automatically have leadership qualities, who are willing to work hard and try new things, who take leadership on their own." One teacher revealed, "It puts a lot of pressure on us. All of the other area schools are looking at us to see how successful we are. They ask, 'How do you do that, because we'd like to do it, too.' We are the first to get up and try it. Also, the school board and administration believe in us."

Teacher leaders in these schools were respected and spoke with confidence. "The teachers here support me because I'm the veteran. I'm coaching others, I'm firm, I'm straight and I'm fair. I'm pretty well respected and I think I'm needed here. Yes, ma'am! That's why I haven't left." When the introduction of schoolwide portfolio assessment was put on hold, one teacher implemented the assessment on her own. She stated, "I need to get started. I've got to be the first one to try it." As her students were creating their own portfolios, the teacher across the hall saw what she was doing and said to others, "You'd better come and see. She's out in the halls talking about it." One teacher simply echoed, "These people who are leaders, you will find that they are outstanding in their field. They excel at whatever they're doing." In one particular school, leadership was viewed on many levels:

> There are academic leaders who really delve into their subject areas and really know it well, and people look up to them for it. [They] go to conferences and bring it all back and share the information. There's the social/emotional angle. They're buzzing around making sure they make connections each day. They keep the ball rolling and keep everybody happy. They enjoy being onstage and we love it! Then there are leaders that keep the whole educational system working well; they're organized and get people behind them to get support in certain areas. We also have our curriculum leaders who work hard to keep us on task, up-to-date, if not ahead of the game. Then [there are] our quiet leaders who do their work humbly and honestly, but people are aware of all they do.

In these change-ready schools, teachers focused early on building capacity in new staff. For instance, one teacher stressed that "the Leadership Team is a two-year commitment and teachers look forward to their terms. This is so important to our school that we have our new teacher sit in on a meeting during her orientation." This teacher reflected on her third term. "It is probably time to give someone else an opportunity to serve because it is a good way, especially for new teachers in the building, to learn a lot about the school." In these schools, teacher leaders and administrators guided each other and served as role models, even promoting student leadership. In one case, a teacher shared that "teachers teach the students to lead one another, so there's a bunch of leaders in our school." Another teacher concurred. "It's not like a leadership hat that's passed around; it's worn at all times by anyone who wants it."

SHARING POWER, AUTHORITY, AND RESPONSIBILITY

In schools initiating efforts to share power, authority, and responsibility, a natural progression of efforts was evident. In the beginning, schools established committees, yet despite good intentions, at times failed to make them as functional as planned. This was exemplified when one teacher remarked, "I think I am on the attendance committee. I mean, I think we have different committees. I know we do, but I have not been on the campus planning committee as far as that goes." Also, teachers acknowledged the commitment of time that committee work required. A committee member commented,

> Most decisions are made in the Leadership Team. Representatives attend from each grade level, including paraprofessionals and others. They meet twice per month. Big concerns are setting goals, checking on those goals and achieving them, [and dealing with] the budget, book adoptions, and renovations. They are also involved in hiring and prioritizing which grade levels need teachers. It is quite a commitment of time.

Although these were important decisions that needed to be addressed, most teachers believed that Leadership Teams needed to focus on what matters most—student learning, that is, "to move away from all the issues of managing and get to the issues of teaching and learning."

Leadership in the initiation stage was, in many cases, limited to those in administrative roles who had earned the respect of their staff. "I guess our principal would be the #1 leader. She supports us. I see a partnership between the assistant and her—a dual relationship." A teacher in another building echoed,

> I think she is a very strong leader. She seems to have a clear vision of what she wants to do. We also have team leaders that go through the assistant

principal to the principal. She [the principal] is a good listener. I don't think she's forgotten what it's like to be in the classroom.

Empowered teachers, however, revealed a sense of autonomy, even at the district level where teacher input was encouraged. "This year all of our staff development is campus-based. Other years it was a mix between district and campus. Usually the district provides us with a menu you can choose from or you can do something that is especially important for you or your team."

Teachers indicated they were listened to at all levels of the organization. "I think everybody feels that they have a right to have input. It lets everybody take ownership and I don't think anybody is afraid of administration stepping on their feet and saying, 'no, you can't do that' because they seem open to anything that's going to benefit kids." Another teacher maintained that "when they [administrators] listen to you, you have some ownership of the school, instead of just following orders. So that is going to motivate you to keep working hard and try new things." Finally, in one school, a faculty council was established and met once a month to discuss concerns and major decisions that the faculty would need to make together.

> The administrators will ask our opinions. They'll make the final decision, but will listen to us. It's usually volunteers. Two middle school teachers chair the council and any teachers who want to come, can. We have a great turnout; just about all the teachers are there. Teachers make up the agenda themselves, so that it's generated from the classroom up. Administration sits with us. Not everybody walks away happy, but everybody feels like they had their say.

Teachers across schools commented on meaningful opportunities to work in small groups before taking their questions, concerns, and ideas to the whole school, "We'll try it out and come up with a solution and then present it to the faculty as a whole to see what everybody else thinks. We have quite a few small groups that do various tasks and work this way." One group for instance, took over the decision to implement a year-round school. It was stated that "the most important part of the decision is the process. It's how the teachers studied the issue, got input from parents and the community, took the information to the school board and finally made the decision. They accepted that responsibility."

At times, individual teachers stepped forward and assumed more responsibility, while in other cases leadership was more collective. Two examples illustrate this point. One teacher stated, "I am mainly here to facilitate. I'm not there to tell them how it should be done—that's not what my role is at all—but to steer them in the right direction. They make the decisions as a group. It's a collaborative effort. The second example was expressed from a principal's viewpoint.

> They're willing to share what they're doing and I'm blessed overall with a very competent faculty. They know we've tried new things and they'll ask to observe others and bring [ideas] back to their classrooms. I feel many teachers are leaders, but it's about leading by example as opposed to [the notion that] you need to be doing this in your classroom.

Schools functioning at higher levels of implementation viewed leadership as pervasive. "We all share leadership. We meet once a week and take turns leading our meetings and take turns being part of the Leadership Team. I think it gives everybody the feeling of being just a little bit more in control and aware of what's going on. From my standpoint, we have a say in how the school should be run." And from another school: "Our principal gives us responsibility, so that we feel a valued part of what's happening. Before, I just did what I was told. . . . I just stayed in my classroom . . . but I didn't feel like I had any impact at the school level. Now I feel more involved."

A curriculum specialist who had been leading the school in a Standards program shared a detailed process:

> When the program started we brought in representatives from each grade level to formulate a plan to talk about standards: what it meant to have standards, how that would impact learning and be the pioneers—to go out into the field and look at the whole process. They met with representatives from other feeder schools and the high school because as a middle school it didn't make sense to do something different from the high school and other feeder schools. Their input and participation was vital for some of the decisions that were coming down.

Finally, an elementary teacher spoke to the heart of shared responsibility. "I think when we realize that the child is the priority, whatever we try needs to help the student and better our school and keep looking forward to the future." Another teacher was concerned about maintaining progress and reacted to the absence of the principal: "She has been instrumental in getting so many things going, but because we now have the tools, I do think we would continue [without her]. We are such a close, personal group that we don't want to go back to where we were."

BROAD-BASED DECISION MAKING
REFLECTING COMMITMENT AND ACCOUNTABILITY

Over time, as teachers become more involved in decision-making processes, they grew in their overall sense of commitment and accountability for student learning. In many cases, teachers came to believe that they were listened to and their opinions were valued. Nonetheless, others argued, "We kept thinking we were going to get to talk about the issues, but decisions are made without a lot of input. We have yet to be provided with an opportunity to brainstorm and try to improve the situation." Another teacher reiterated, "I don't feel like I ever had any real say-so as far as the inservice. I was told I didn't have an option; you were just going to do this."

As schools consciously guided their efforts to create PLCs, participatory decision-making structures were developed that sought representation from all areas: teachers, counselors, parents, community members, and administrators, often elected by the faculty members in each school. Depending on the decisions, even students were empowered to make building-level decisions in some cases. "At times we've even been strong enough to let the kids make a decision, and we, the faculty, look at them and go, oh, what a great idea! Maybe we should go along with it. So we've been on the reciprocal end of leadership as well."

Despite efforts at developing inclusive and diverse teams, one comment indicated how easy it was to neglect an important entity: "The only thing I see that doesn't work sometime is the paraprofessionals. They don't have a vote in the Leadership Team and sometimes they're not given the information or they're given it secondhand." Yet, for the most part, broad representation was evident. "In addition to the teacher representatives, a paraprofessional attends, also one building administrator, an administrator from the central office, a business person, a parent, and a neighborhood representative." She added, "In the Leadership Team we talk about issues, we have the opportunity to express our opinions, and major decisions are made. Grade-level representatives take notes, and we go over them in grade-level meetings the next day."

In general, teachers indicated that decision-making processes had changed significantly over the past two years of the project, "This year I see a lot of change. Administrators now sit down and talk to us, even if it's after school. We'll meet for five minutes and they'll tell us what's going on and ask us what we think. This is a big change from when we didn't even know what was happening." Teachers told stories about redesigning job descriptions, reviewing and setting schedules, and planning staff development sessions for a greater impact on student learning.

Nonetheless, shared decision making has not evolved without some difficulty. "We talk about things and we're sometimes on two different ends of the spectrum, but we bounce it back and forth. Ok, girls! We can't reach a decision. Let's talk about it, think about it. By such and such a meeting we're gong to vote and we do. Sometimes it's a little controversial." Another teacher revealed, "There's always one decision that you're not comfortable with or you don't care for it. But the job's got to get done. Compromises simply have to be made."

Although district and building administrators make the "big decisions," teachers expressed that they could share their feelings about various situations and offer alternative ways of doing things. "I'm not really aware of just how much our teacher decisions influence the 'big decisions' that need to be made. There are times it's not practical for teacher opinions to matter." It seemed acceptable that teachers' ideas were not always acted upon, as long as they were heard. Depending on the issue, teachers accepted the fact that some decisions needed to be made by board members and administrators, while others could be made by team leaders, whole staffs, or in teams. "Sometimes my grade-level team has the freedom to make decisions on how we run our government, how we make rules for a study hall [and so forth], so there are different levels of decisions being made by almost everybody." As one teacher insisted, "Site-based committees make decisions that our principal is a part of and teachers are a part of, community members are a part of, parents—all help with decision making."

It was commonly reported that classroom teachers made most decisions that affected children. More than one teacher claimed, "Our principal calls us together in our groups, allows us to have input into what's needed and what's best for the child. We interact with each other and solve problems to help the children." In one school, if children were experiencing academic or behavioral problems, teachers would refer them to the building-level committee chair [a teacher] and the necessary procedures were followed to assure that students' needs were met. Another teacher captured the bottom line:

When it involves the children and if it's something that can be changed and is not mandated from the central office or by the state or whatever, I think the administrators get together with the teachers who are leaders and make those kinds of decisions. If they think it's something that can be changed, the teachers' voices can be heard.

The majority of curricular decisions "were made by teachers who were willing to take some risks and try new things." These decisions involve when and what will be taught and in what kinds of ways. Teachers acknowledged that in some cases it would be easier if someone else would make the decision, for example, when deciding whether chapter reading programs should be campuswide or self-contained. A teacher stated,

It was completely the teachers' decision. We had always been told this is the way we're going to do it; now it was happening. The site-based committees helped that, where teachers have a lot more input. It's good because it's not handed down from the top, because sometimes the top doesn't know what the bottom is doing.

One teacher indicated that the school had site-based committees for a variety of functions. "Often the committee will make a presentation and then take a poll, take opinions, and discuss it that way. Other times, the committee will meet with the principal or simply by themselves. I don't know of a way that it could be more organized. I would say it's delegated very fairly."

In general, teachers revealed they had a voice within their role. "Even as a classroom teacher, my opinions are valued. I may not always get my way on something, but they [the administration] listen. They are supportive and

I feel I'm part of the decision-making process." This was important as most schools had many people involved in developing their campus plans. One teacher maintained, "We were all there. It was an open discussion and we said okay, on this page and section we're going to change this and this. Do you agree with this or do you not agree with it? And so the whole staff— the teachers and the aides—were there." Another teacher reflected, "I think as long as we're a learning community, it's improving our school."

In PLCs, principals are not coercive or controlling, but seek to share power and distribute leadership among staff. In turn, staff increasingly become open to changing roles and responsibilities. Principals let go of power and nurture the human side and expertise of the entire school community. Shared responsibility is apparent through broad-based decision making that reflects commitment and accountability.

4

Shared Values and Vision

Among the key features of a school community is a core of shared values about what students should learn, about how faculty and students should behave, and about the shared aims to maintain community.

—Karen Seashore Louis and Sharon D. Kruse, *Professionalism and Community: Perspectives on Reforming Urban Schools*

Staff shares values and visions for school improvement based on student needs and high expectations. Shared vision reflects norms of behavior that guide decisions about teaching and learning.

ESPOUSED VALUES AND NORMS

Recognition and consideration of values and beliefs often guide decisions for schools. One example reflects a critical value across all dimensions—trust. A veteran teacher described interactions among faculty: "To develop a 'living' curriculum you have to have trust with your faculty members that they are teaching what they are supposed to teach." In another school, trust was also very important: "You must have trust in each other to do whatever you can to help that person and know that they will help you." In one school, trust was just developing: "We are trying to build some comfort zones where teachers can come out and say 'gosh this isn't working for me.'"

There are other examples of shared values that guide instructional decisions. One principal explained:

> I think you might be hearing a very good interaction between teachers and students. Certainly you would hear teachers listening as well as talking. You would see kids interacting very easily with teachers. It is very much a give-and-take kind of situation. It seems very friendly.

In another school the staff considered ways to balance content and relationships for the benefit of the students.

> Kids are treated with respect and they know they have a place to learn. They also get the material they need to be successful at the next level so they can succeed. We try to change as fast as we need to so we develop the balance between relational teaching and getting the content to the students.

In another school, a teacher commented on the importance of values for the teachers and students.

> Values are taught everyday here—like honesty, perseverance, helpfulness, and consideration. That's the kind of values they need. I think if they can see the teachers being considerate to one another and having fun and enjoying what they are doing, it shows children hard work can be fun. It can be worth it.

At the initiation level, the development of these shared values leads teachers and administrators to create common norms of behavior that hope to become lived and embedded in the culture of the school. These norms can be written or unwritten and formalized into rituals and ceremonies that occur regularly in the school. These expected ways of interacting provide a safe environment where students and teachers look forward to engaging in supported learning.

STAFF SHARE A SCHOOL VISION
FOCUSED ON STUDENT LEARNING

In many schools, while the intent of the teachers and administrators centered on what is best for students, the vision statement was vague. "I think all teachers just value the chance for children to come and learn. Everybody's on a different level but we realize that and we're trying to get everybody to that goal," commented one teacher. Another teacher also expressed a desire to help children:

> I'm still willing to change and get out of the box and try new things if I think it's going to benefit the children. That's what we're here for. I think our goal as teachers is to make sure that our children leave us with knowledge that they didn't know before they came to us. And, hopefully as they progress in the years, they'll get in real-life situations and apply what they've learned at school.

In some schools, however, teachers are not clear about the vision or how it was developed. "I don't know what the vision statement is—it just wasn't something important for me to remember. I remember meetings when it was discussed, but I don't recall necessarily if I had input. I'm sure I could have had input if I had wanted it." Another teacher, who saw limitations as barriers to developing a common vision, commented, "I think as a school we are doing the best we know how, with the funding we received, I think we're right on track as far as getting our children to where we [want them to be]. We're doing as much as we can do." Other teachers noted the role of the administration. For instance,

> Administrators see the big picture, whereas we have tunnel vision. I see what's appropriate to my classroom. I know that when push comes to shove, I have to bow to their discretion and have confidence that they see that big picture. Even if I don't see them all the time, I'm involved and I'm supported. I'd feel very comfortable standing up and opposing something that was proposed if I really had an opposition to it.

A reflective teacher observed that changes were being made that improved the process of getting focused. She stated, "It is seeming a bit more focused. Last year we were way too scattered. And now we are trying to be more focused—maybe choose three or four things instead of going all over the place."

Only one school developed its vision statement and plan by involving all stakeholders. "I think we had all faculty in the beginning. We also had representation from the janitors, carpenters, parents, school board members, and community people. There were a lot of people giving ideas and we came up with a plan."

Several schools expressed a common vision regarding student success.

> We feel that every child will be successful, feel important, and feel like they're learning something. Lately we have discovered that this is possible through a lot of things we've been doing with inclusion. It is becoming a lot easier to realize that this is an attainable goal—that every kid can succeed.

Another school related the common vision to curriculum. "We are always refocusing our vision. We look at our curriculum and we look at what is coming down the pike—like portfolio assessment for students and teachers. So we look to the future, determine our weaknesses, and work to develop strengths."

HIGH EXPECTATIONS

Setting expectations often begins with the principal, but in the high-readiness schools at the implementation phase, the teachers quickly assumed the responsibility for continuing to develop and to sustain those expectations. Thus, in implementing the shared vision, teachers held themselves to high expectations. One teacher maintained, "There is just no end to what we're doing in the learning community. I don't think we're ever going to stop changing." Another teacher continued, "We're committed to helping each individual child to achieve the best education he can."

Central office support is needed for teachers to continue to learn and grow so they can reach those high expectations. One teacher noted, "I would say that our school system values the increasing intellectual capacities of the teachers. And they offer us many opportunities to learn new skills and new ideas and how to better serve our kids."

SHARED VISION GUIDES
TEACHING AND LEARNING

Once student focus is established, schools develop decisions regarding implementation of the vision. Regarding her school's plan, one teacher explained, "I think that student learning would be most important and getting the students prepared for the next level of learning. We do that by working together and consulting with one another." One school attributed the success of their efforts to staff cohesiveness. "When we made our improvement plan, and when we implement our plan, we always go back to our togetherness and our support of all the staff and the administration."

One school designed a process to develop a vision and monitor progress with the entire school community every semester.

> We had a staff meeting prior to the break and the principal laid down the rules and expectations. From that meeting we chose categories that we needed to work on—behavior and academic. We developed committees to work on those two areas and we came up with a plan to look at what we could do to implement change. Then we were given a time to get back together to present so that we could all be on the same page.

Staying "on the same page" is a challenge for many teachers, as reflected by this quote: "I can go out and do my own planning, but I have to have some validation from the group. If I don't have that, then we are not having the systematic application that we are looking for as a group."

Some schools strive to get their message out to the larger community. A principal lamented, "We know it is important to get our message out. We've tried it in several ways—we send notes home, we send invitations to parents to come see what we're doing, we try to get info into the newspaper—but we feel like we still haven't hit the right key yet." Another principal described a more systematic way to communicate the vision. "There is a monthly newsletter and something is always written about what is happening in the classroom. In addition, the Talented and Gifted class is developing a web page [that] will include interviews with teachers about what is taking place in the classes." These interviews show the significance of parent and community involvement in developing the vision and implementing relevant curricular programs that support students' learning and school improvement.

Structures must be in place that embrace and build upon "lived" rather than simply espoused values that focus on continuous learning for students and staff. Moreover, visions that are co-created and purposeful are most effective in mobilizing commitment and ownership among all involved in the teaching and learning process. A vision that is not built on shared values lacks heart and, ultimately, will be ineffective in guiding efforts.

5

Collective Learning and Application

It is the teachers' responsibility to engage in collaborative learning with other teachers, principals, parents, and students, to achieve the shared purpose; and to take collective responsibility for student learning.

—Fred Newmann and Gary Wehlage,
Successful School Restructuring

Staff at all levels of the school share information and work collaboratively to plan, solve problems, and improve learning opportunities. Together they seek knowledge, skills, and strategies, and apply what they learn to their work.

SHARING INFORMATION

In the early phase—initiation—of professional learning community development, establishing a school culture that values sharing information is critical. Too often we continue to see teachers hoarding materials and reluctant to enter into any kind of collaboration with other teachers. School leadership, including principals, department chairs, team leaders, and other teacher leaders, must be proactive in modeling collaborative behavior and in supporting colleagues—norms to be embedded into the culture. In one school a veteran teacher reflected on sharing information:

> There are a lot of good people willing to share their insights, knowledge, and information. You gain a lot of strength because you hear what everybody said, then you have the benefit of the older teachers' knowledge and the benefit of the newer teachers—new classes, new direction. So that's been real good.

Another teacher explained the value of sharing and how that impacts the relationships in the school:

> We share information from the first day when we begin looking at the scope and sequence. As the year goes on, we revisit and share new information. We discuss what happens in the leadership team and good ideas that teachers have. The most important part about teaching is your relationship with your peers and your ability to share, have fun, and learn from each other.

The issue of time negatively impacted opportunities for teachers to generate questions and share ideas. In one school, time appeared as a nonexemplar and hindered communication. "We really don't have time to visit someone else. That would require a sub or someone to cover, and while we want to do this, the opportunity just hasn't been available." Regarding time, this teacher explained, "We want to make changes in the units we are teaching, yet it is hard to find time to have that collaborative effort. That's probably our biggest difficulty." However, in another school, the principal scheduled meetings designed to increase the possibility of sharing information and providing time for dialogue:

> There are many opportunities for them to share in grade-level meetings each week. The meeting after LT [leadership team] is sharing administrative information, and the meeting the other week deals more with instructional issues. Faculty meetings are twice a month on Thursdays after school.

In some cases, the conversation reflected diverse viewpoints. One teacher described a situation in which people respected each other's opinions, but struggled to reach consensus: "There are strong opinions and we listen, we serve as a sounding board to each other, and we brainstorm. We see another side, we step back, get another perspective, and sometimes our opinions are changed."

SEEKING NEW KNOWLEDGE, SKILLS, AND STRATEGIES

Gaining knowledge, skills, and strategies often is accomplished by traditional staff development, including workshops, mini-workshops, conferences, district inservices, and university courses. At one school there were several choices. "Some staff development days are site- or district-determined. Other times we decide as a staff what new learning we want, and who we want to present. Some years we have book studies." In another school much of the learning occurred in the grade-level teams. "We did a workshop for some of our teachers on writing lesson plans. We share and learn from each other through our grade-level meetings and workshops."

Another group of teachers responded to an opportunity they had to attend Eric Jensen's presentation on brain research. Returning from the experience "motivated and enthusiastic," approximately 20 teachers met after school over a period of a month at various teachers' homes to discuss the experience and his book. One teacher shared,

No one in particular led the group. Each week we had a different format. We would talk about different aspects and then divide into groups. Each time we'd be with different people, which was nice. More often than not, we discussed what we were supposed to have read for that week, then come together to talk about it further. We'd meet up to four hours a session.

As staff learned new skills and strategies, often they would be concerned about classroom application. One program that assisted one school's faculty in program implementation was described this way: "It is a structured activity where I can present something and get some constructive feedback in a nonthreatening environment." Another teacher explained how her team implemented new learning: "We meet almost every day for about 40 to 45 minutes. We talk about what we are doing in class and how we can modify our lessons."

In one school the faculty members were working on team teaching. They were trying to form student teams in each other's classrooms. The social studies teacher commented, "The students did a writing assignment and I graded it on content, and the writing teacher graded it on style. We try to get them to see things across the board. It works well. We are trying to do more hands-on activities after the lecturing."

COLLABORATIVE WORK TO PLAN, SOLVE PROBLEMS, AND IMPROVE LEARNING OPPORTUNITIES

Regarding the ability to work together, in the schools just beginning the professional learning community approach, a teacher commented, "It's hard to believe that we are so isolated. We would be working next door to someone and you don't see them or talk with them."

Collaborative planning efforts in the schools in the implementation phase ranged from very few to highly integrated. One teacher described the progression:

> I think it was a gradual process. To begin with we were very isolated—she planned, and I planned. Then we began to work together and to talk. Then we started to plan together as a grade level. Then we started to work together as staff. It has been real gradual.

Another teacher reinforced this collaboration. "We started talking to teachers in other grades and we found ourselves headed in the same direction. We're all very individual with our own strengths and weaknesses, but when you plan together, you gain a lot of insight." Another teacher discussed the planning efforts in his school:

> You are always doing team stuff, in one way or another—preparing something for your team, meeting with your team, or being in on a student intervention team meeting. So our planning periods here are seen a lot differently than in some schools where you are hidden in a room correcting papers. We collaborate a lot more during our planning time during the day.

Schools that were successful in collective problem solving generally had a process in place to deal systematically with issues. One secondary school delegated problem solving to committees. "We usually meet a couple times a year in large groups to focus on several issues. Then schoolwide decisions are made and from there, several committees are assigned tasks to work on throughout the year." One elementary teacher described the process more informally: "In my LT [leadership team] we took a few minutes and had the primary people explain to the middle school people what the issue is. Then we questioned them as to what the problems were, and they solved some of their problems by just talking about them."

Describing the process for resolving issues at the team level, one teacher stated, "Our team is especially close. We work well together and get insight, help, and suggestions from each other. If we have a problem with a student, we open the door and ask for help or for that student to go to that teacher's room." Many teachers described opportunities they experienced to improve learning at their schools. One kindergarten teacher explained that the team was working hard to provide consistency in the curriculum. "We're really trying to unify together. We are still building, but we see it and it's connecting. We have to work together, all of us."

An emerging sense of teamwork contributed to teachers' feelings of autonomy. Teachers indicated that they meet as a team and discuss various issues. For example, one teacher explained, "Right now as the social studies team, we're trying to come up with a curriculum. We put in our bid for what we would like our schedule to be and we help one another." In another school that had just received parent approval for starting an alternative program for at-risk learners, one teacher shared,

> We developed a curriculum and put together a different program that would best meet the needs of these kids. We developed a one-year pilot to see how it all works this year. Then we have to report to the school board once every two months, and give a report of how things are going.

Another teacher revealed the method the principal used to develop the school improvement plan. "We have a faculty meeting when we give input in each area of the plan. We could suggest new areas, change wording, or add ways that we implement the plan. We also have access to the data to make better decisions."

Even though there were many examples of collaboration within schools, some teachers felt the district could support their efforts more effectively. "The district is getting better in scheduling our time. We are having more time in our departments during inservice days instead of meeting as one big faculty group. It's hard to get things done when you're in a big group." It is clear that district support was needed to assist each school in achieving its targeted goals as related to the specific school improvement plan.

For school improvement plans to be effective, it is imperative for the entire school community to take responsibility for sharing information and working collaboratively to solve critical problems affecting student learning. It is also essential that staff continue to learn by collectively seeking knowledge and skills and applying new learning to their practice.

6

Shared Personal Practice

This means that teachers work diligently, practice in exemplary ways, keep abreast of new ideas, and help other members of the learning community be successful.

—Thomas J. Sergiovanni, *Moral Leadership*

Peers visit with and observe one another to offer encouragement and to provide feedback on instructional practices to assist in student achievement and increase individual and organizational capacity.

PEERS VISIT AND OBSERVE
TO OFFER ENCOURAGEMENT

Many interviews illustrated the occurrence of teachers meeting and sharing information while offering support. One teacher explained, "I meet with the other eighth-grade teachers, and we brainstorm and we do our observations and share ideas." In another school, small planning committees meet, and then they "all meet together and share between the groups. We meet at least on a weekly basis." However, teachers did not visit other teachers in all schools. "We visited at the beginning of the year, but unfortunately we've slacked off." In another school, one teacher did not see how she could visit other classrooms because she teaches a self-contained classroom all day.

One school had structured peer observations. "We go into each other's classrooms and we do a peer observation. We have one due every nine weeks. You actually go in and observe the class and write up what you observe. Then after class you discuss it with them."

Collaboration and sharing appeared to be the norm, and at one elementary school a teacher expressed that "My partner and I switch classes during our planning periods two days a week. It works perfectly for us because we have the same students."

However, in another school, informality is the standard procedure. One school was built as an open concept building to enhance communication and proximity. Teachers shared a wall between classrooms, and there were front and back doors for teachers to travel in and out of throughout the day. "For instance, my team partner is a first-year teacher and we leave our door open all the time. So if she has questions about something, she just runs through and says, 'What do I do?' In fact, most of our doors stay open." This school was also arranged to allow the content mastery room to back up to their resource room, where the teachers in both areas "had a lot of common children and used common strategies." Grade-level classrooms were also connected so, for instance, a third-grade teacher can go next door and ask the second-grade teacher what was taught the year before. In schools with a less facilitative structure, teachers have a specific day and time to meet; however, when they were asked about times to meet, they said, "In the course of a day we meet two or three times. Because we are situated close to one another, we are in constant contact."

FEEDBACK TO IMPROVE
INSTRUCTIONAL PRACTICE

Regarding specific classroom issues, one teacher commented, "I say to my partner, 'You know I need help with so-and-so. Are you having problems or do you know something that will work?'" One teacher who used a more individualized observation approach throughout the school year noted:

I chose a teacher and observed her during my off period. Then I took notes and made comments on how she presented her lesson. I knew she was good at what she did and I wanted to try to get a few tips from her. I learned a few strategies and her approach to different things. I was impressed. She did a good job.

A few schools reported that teachers share classrooms or a team together. A teacher in one school explained, "Some of us get the luxury of having another teacher working with us in the classroom. And depending on which teacher you work with, you dovetail it differently, and the students see the model of people respecting each other." Other teachers, regardless of experience, support one another with regard to individual students.

If there's a disciplinary problem and another teacher just needs to take five, she'll send them to our room and we just work with the child. We do that a lot to help out in the disciplinary areas. The team really gets together and works on that. Our teams also work across grade levels to get insight from each other, help, and suggestions.

For one teacher, problems are often not addressed. "If I need to talk to other teachers, I can try to find someone who has the same off period that I have. Otherwise, I just deal with it."

In several schools the feedback is more general and covers information that can help the teachers develop and the school improve. One school organized an all-day meeting where outstanding teachers talked with newer teachers. "The team explained things the teachers would be going through during the year—grade books, classroom management, [and so forth]." Another school also had teacher planning days each month.

We do different things schoolwide. All the teachers and aides come in. We just all have a great time. It's fun to just get together in a no-pressure environment and learn something that we can take back and implement in our classrooms.

SHARING OUTCOMES OF
INSTRUCTIONAL PRACTICE

In one district, once a month teachers from primary and middle schools came together to talk about dilemmas and possible solutions. They also brought in and shared student work to offer suggestions as to how they could improve it in the class. A second-grade team met to look at student work and discovered alternative ways to teach. One teacher remarked, "This is an eye-opener. I didn't think to teach it this way." At another school, review of student work was emphasized during parent visits.

At times, a change in practice was sparked by frustration. The teachers in a third-grade team were discouraged with their phonics program. They consulted with the second-grade teachers and talked with their principal to get background information. Then they met as a team, analyzed their students' work, and determined it would be in the students' best interest to make a change in their approach to the phonics program.

At the secondary level, English teachers would collectively review students' writing samples to help them revise their writing so that they would be more successful on the end-of-school writing exams and college placement tests.

COACHING AND MENTORING

In some schools, coaching and mentoring have moved beyond traditional, summative assessment models to coaching activities and interactions that serve to develop and sustain real professional growth. Teacher-to-teacher mentoring takes place, for example, when teachers are teaching outside their certification or teaching a new preparation and veteran teachers offer assistance in sharing school policy and practice. In the following situation, the veteran teacher mentored a teacher new to the building: "This is how I do it with my class. You can modify—but I am going to help you out." Another teacher coached a beginning teacher and described her progress, "She is moving so quickly. . . . She has her grade book set up with benchmarks, and is very organized. She is a young teacher, but people are going to her and asking her how to prepare the grade book program."

From the new teacher's perspective, the coaching she received was valued. In describing the coach, she said, "She was able to relate to me and give me feedback. I was nervous at first when she came in, but when it was over with, and after she talked with me, I was a lot closer to her. She told me what was good, how I might change some things, and it helped me improve what I was doing."

Other teams begin mentoring each other from the first of the year. "We check with each other from the start to see if we have materials and are teaching what is expected by the district. Each of us has strengths. It is good to have the in-flow of the new teachers as well as the veteran teachers. It is a good mix."

Through all of the shared personal practice examples, it was apparent that developing a trusting relationship was the first step for successful interaction. A teacher explained, "We are becoming more willing to share with each other. That is part of what I think is helping to build a trusting atmosphere. We borrow and revise all the time. People are very accepting of suggestions." In addition to developing trust, staff clearly must share and provide feedback on instructional practices to achieve improvements in student achievement.

7

Supportive Conditions

Current conditions in the schools—the isolation, the difficulty in assessing one's effectiveness as a teacher, the lack of collegial and administrative support, and the sense of powerlessness that comes from limited collegial decision-making make it difficult for teachers to maintain a strong sense of efficacy.

—Patricia Ashton, "Teacher Efficacy: A Motivational Paradigm for Effective Teacher Education," *Journal of Teacher Education*

Collegial relationships include respect, trust, norms of critical inquiry and improvement, and positive, caring relationships among students, teachers, and administrators. *Structures* include a variety of conditions such as size of the school, proximity of staff to one another, communication systems, and the time and space for staff to meet and examine current practices.

COLLEGIAL RELATIONSHIPS

Creating a readiness for change is critical and often does not occur without focusing on the people in the organization and the interaction among all stakeholders. Some call it the human side of change, which is critical in establishing the culture of the school. All schools in the study were diligent in their efforts to increase trust and respect, provide emotional and tangible support among staff, and focus where it mattered by engaging staff, and in some cases the greater school community, in critical inquiry and school improvement.

Administrators were not only approachable, but helped to create a climate of trust and respect, which for some principals required more change than others. One teacher noted, "In the beginning he was very opposed to a lot of change. Now he's used to it. Change is just a normal everyday fact of life here because it's constantly evolving. That only happens when there is a lot of trust and he has an excellent staff here." Regarding the same principal two years later, it was reported that

> He puts a lot of trust into these people and the fact that they will be able to carry things off and do whatever makes him look good. He's definitely changed. He's worked to build trust. Whatever he expects you to do, he follows up on it to see your progress and check to see what other resources you need. That's the number one help as an administrator, and it also keeps him in touch with what's going on.

A middle school teacher reflected on support of a new principal and revealed, "I now have someone who's open to working with me, who values my contribution. And that's good, and better than what it was. That's what teachers need to have."

Another teacher noted the type of rapport that was most commonly shared. "You're very comfortable talking with her. She's not like a principal. She's more like your fellow worker, or at least she makes you feel that way." Staff efforts were recognized as evident in this comment: "Our principal and vice principal are really good for me. If we do anything, they take note of it and give us a good compliment. I feel comfortable with the fact that I can go to either and talk to them about anything, and they would give their best to help me solve problems."

A majority of teachers indicated that there were few problems that they couldn't discuss with their administrators because they weren't afraid of repercussions or conflict. As one teacher stated, "If we hit a brick wall, he'll be there to say we need to talk to this person about whatever, or he'll go with you and break new ground or open doors so you can take your ideas a step further." In terms of what's important, in the eyes of one teacher, it was fairness: "I feel like I'm treated fairly and I feel like we treat the students fairly and being fair means everyone has a voice. It's not a dictatorship. It's just fair . . . to the students, the teachers, the administrators and the parents."

Further, teachers enjoyed sharing with their administrators and being made to feel important, which was evident in the following two sentiments:

> I'm working on a special project with my team that Jean is letting us do. I'm sure when we bring it to her, she will look at it and say it looks great. She's very attuned. Though she hasn't worked in a classroom setting for a while, she's still eager. When we have fresh ideas, she's eager to hear all about them. She carries them to other administrators and says this is what my teachers want.

The second teacher was made to feel like he made a difference and stated, "He [the principal] understands it's the teacher who really has the real impact. He values and supports what the faculty does, what they say. He does a real good job of including the faculty in making the decisions that are really going to affect student achievement." Similarly, at another school, a teacher stated, "People are valued and are made to feel they are making a difference. There's mutual respect between our role as a teacher and how that fits into the district roles and district curriculum." And yet another teacher asserted, "We have the final say in what we teach and how we teach it. That's a lot of trust right there. Giving us that reign really helps us to develop the relationship."

One teacher revealed that when trust is dishonored, "to rebuild it, you have to talk to those individuals that you've offended, face-to-face and really put it out there. If you really mean it, you have to show by your words and actions. But if you try to do it through others or try to skirt the issue or ignore it, then the word gets out and that's not good."

Colleagues were also viewed as a significant source of support to one another. "My fellow teachers support me the most. If I'm not sure about something I know, then I can go to those teachers. I can trust them to give me the right information and guide me as to how to get further information." Another thought was, "I can be honest and say this isn't working for me and won't feel betrayed or made to feel foolish." Staff also become close through regularly scheduled meetings, whether by grade-level teams or Leadership Teams:

I've gone through divorces in that group. It's more than just a group who work together, it's become a family. You find out some pretty personal things about people when you're meeting that often, especially if it's been stressful for them, they share a lot. It's really become a close-knit group and you become protective of one another.

A veteran maintained that the individuals on her team were her best collegial support: "We're all working with the same kids and can share the same concerns. I've been on teams that have worked very well because the teachers listen and respect each other and accept each other without judgment." In a similar light, a new teacher shared her appreciation of the veteran teachers in her school, who "took me under their wings. You can go to all the teacher orientations in the world, but there's nothing like that firsthand experience. They nurtured me and carried me, and told me what I could do to improve." It seemed that the team spirit transferred to students. "Our students have become more loving, more at ease with each other, at ease with themselves. Their self-esteem has gone up. They seem to be feeling less pressure to learn and succeed. The pressure for us is preparing students for the state test." Another teacher added, "If we recognize that our students perform better in a more communicative and trusting environment, then it only makes sense that the staff would as well."

STRUCTURES

DuFour and Eaker (1998) argued that structures are critical in cultivating the culture of a school. Whether the issue is time, a problem endemic in our schools today; proximity and communication; or effective mechanisms to engage staff in meaningful dialogue, these six schools are working impressively to overcome obstacles to change.

Interestingly enough, the issue of time was addressed quite differently across schools. At the initiation stage, some staff could not get past the antiquated structures that have deterred progress through the years, while in other schools the staff attacked the issue with hope and creativity. Still, teachers criticized any unproductive use of time. "I wish things weren't so piecemeal. My impression is that at times it's hit or miss." More often it was felt that administrators and leadership teams were working on rearranging or buying time. One teacher confessed, "A lot of it is that we don't think that we have the time to go out and browse and get information, but I've never been denied anything, that reasonably speaking, I thought would benefit my class." Often it was noted that teachers would be given subs, which they "figured was money well spent, for instance, "when the seventh-grade social studies teachers got subs for a couple days and we got to work on six-week unit tests together. We all had to give the same test, so we needed time to actually develop it."

In all six schools, collaboration was the norm:

It's nice to have time set aside to talk with other English teachers. Good teachers will make time. They'll seek out other teachers and ask what they're doing to teach their objectives. They may talk about it over lunch. It's hard to do it after school when, as adults, you always have other things to do. I think a lot of time you wouldn't be collaborating as well with other teachers if you didn't have regular team time. That is what you use your time for.

A middle school curriculum specialist indicated that the focus was on creating situations for professional dialogue and planning around standards and benchmarks.

Planning periods here are seen a lot differently than in most schools where teachers are hidden in their rooms correcting papers. We collaborate a lot more during our planning time around the standards and benchmarks, complex reasoning skills and knowledge construction strategies. As we dialogue, people get more familiar with them and integrate them into their thinking processes.

A colleague added, "There's a lot of time given to us to share ideas and get together. Our day yesterday was fully devoted to unit planning, and that's really special because we can sit down and discuss the direction we are headed [in] with our units and our curriculum." Teachers also find time to meet on a more informal basis. "We don't really have a meeting time; we just see each other and gather together and talk. Sometimes it's social, but we meet constantly to coordinate and discuss facilities, schedules, curriculum, students, beliefs and values. It's good for kids because we pass on our personal values." In this same middle school, 10 minutes were added to each day to schedule two banked days for inservice, days in which staff had ownership in the schedule for the day. "We are trying to keep these days sacred and focused." Another teacher added, "When we don't have common planning time with other grade levels, this time is invaluable to all work together. Otherwise it just doesn't happen. When we get the chance, we are enriched by it. Finding time is really our biggest difficulty."

Grants and building funds were also garnered to provide substitute teachers and small stipends:

> Time is always a factor in whatever you're doing. Giving stipends through our enrichment grant is not ideal, but it helps. With balanced literacy in the primary school, the second-grade teachers had off at the same time and could plan together. That made all the difference. Their learning curve has been real high this year. They are constantly coming up with new ideas, because it made them look at what they were doing. One night they even worked on a literacy library until 9:00 on their own time.

Some participants in the study felt that teachers also have responsibility in making time available to meet. "The flexibility has always been there, but it's not always accessed until you set the stage for teachers and say, 'Gee whiz, we need to do this.' We found we could shift time to make different things happen." These teachers found it was simply a matter of shifting their recess period.

Middle school teachers realized the problems school administrators frequently face when trying to arrange meeting times; however, they actually found a time where teachers could work together in mixed groups after assessing potential problems. "Because we're on different time schedules, we knew if we scheduled it after school, some people would just leave. They wouldn't wait around for another hour to meet. So we did some overlapping which involved stipends that provided incentives."

Principals often found innovative ways to garner resources. For instance, one teacher commented, "When I see something I'm interested in she somehow finds the money." In another school, teachers noted that they were free to observe their peers or other schools at will "to gather effective teaching strategies and see how other teachers structure time." Opportunities for additional training were also noted, even to the degree that, "you'd better be careful what you ask for because you'll get it. Then you can't back down. At almost every staff meeting our principal presents workshops that she encourages us to go to and very seldom are we refused. Somehow she'll find a way for us to go." Another principal is providing time in the summer with Eisenhower money that is normally budgeted for her use. "Now we can have uninterrupted time when school is out. We are going to put as many unit teams together as we can and creatively finance it."

The structures also varied in each facility, but most were created to facilitate collaboration and support. "Our school is structured so that we work in houses on teams. And one of the physical spaces where you can see it is in the teacher-planning center where the desks are actually put together by teams so there is an opportunity for physical proximity for planning, which is always at the same time." One teacher shared how she used her lunch hour and after school to tutor students in her high school, leaving little time to meet with staff: "Just the nature of what we're doing isolates us." Another teacher indicated that teaching eight years in a portable caused her to be "seriously disconnected to the other teachers." Some teachers "just don't see each other. Our schedules are totally different. We don't really socialize or consult each other unless it's at a meeting."

Communication systems varied as well, from morning assemblies with informal chats, e-mail, message boards to enhance two-way communication, notes of recognition, and daily newsletters and memos to minutes of meetings. One teacher praised her school: "I never have to find out about things through the grapevine. I may have to stop in the office and read a message board, but I still know what's going on." In another school, the daily announcements were listed on the back of each teacher's absentee list. "So you save teaching time and it's all there in writing." In other schools, telephones were available in each room for teachers to use to keep the lines of communication open to enhance parent involvement and support. "We find that parents really do want what's best for kids." Another school used a telephone call-in system "where twice a week teachers use the Interlink to share what's happening, like upcoming events. The parents can call in and leave a message or ask questions and the teachers get back to them."

These six schools utilized various methods to communicate with parents and their communities. Moreover, one school invested in a public relations specialist "to get the word out to the community, to put the word in the local paper about the good things that are going on."

In PLCs, daily interactions move beyond caring relationships to higher levels of trust, respect, and recognition. Risk-taking is commonplace as norms encourage collaboration and experimentation. Decision-making structures and visions guide practices that affect student learning. In addition, a united effort from school staff, parents, and community members is critical to embed effective practices and values into the culture of the school.

> The aspect of the workplace—the nature of the professional community that exists there—appears more critical than any other factor to the character of teaching and learning for teachers and their students.
>
> —Milbrey McLaughlin, *What Matters Most in Teachers' Workplace Context*

3

ASSESSING AND RECULTURING SCHOOLS

8

Assessing Schools as PLCs

Dianne F. Olivier

If educators are indeed persuaded that transforming schools into professional learning communities offers the best strategy for school improvement, a clear vision of what a community looks like and how people operate within this community must be established. In order to visualize the culture in which professional learning communities exist, a portrait of learning communities can be sketched by examining the dimensions and critical attributes forming the PLC.

The complexity that exists in identifying schools as PLCs offers a challenge for researchers, principals, staff, parents, and other stakeholders. While many principals and faculties conceptualize their schools as organizations operating as learning communities, they rarely meet the operational criteria. Schools that are operating as professional learning communities must foster a culture in which learning by all is valued, encouraged, and supported. Additionally, within such communities, "the staff, intentionally and collectively, engage in learning and work on issues directly related to classroom practice that positively impacts student learning" (Cowan & Hord, 1999, p. 4). Thus, in assessing the level of progress along a continuum of PLC development, specific school and classroom practices must be measured as determining factors of this development for school renewal.

INITIAL EFFORTS OF ASSESSING SCHOOLS AS PLCS

In our first year of work with Hord at the Southwest Educational Development Laboratory (SEDL), we used the *School Professional Staff as Learning Community* questionnaire (Hord, 1998). This instrument was developed to identify schools as professional learning communities, based on Hord's review of the literature. In Hord's search for PLCs, she requested nominations of such schools; however, the results proved disappointing, which led to the beginning of the SEDL project.

Initial development of an assessment tool to identify school staffs as professional learning communities addressed several needs. Using this instrument, researchers could conduct studies of schools that were clear examples of PLCs while providing information on how a PLC is created. This instrument would also provide baseline data, as well as design a developmental continuum through periodic administration. The measure offered a diagnostic tool to inform studies pertaining to how principals work with staff and how they provide opportunities for continuous learning, interaction, and support. Finally, the assessment tool could provide data during the various phases of change from initiation to implementation to institutionalization.

Hord's instrument comprised 17 descriptors grouped into the five major dimensions. These descriptors defined the dimensions and were designed as a series of three statements structured along a continuum from the most desirable to the least desirable practice of the descriptor. The five-point scale provided for differentiation of the descriptor from high to middle to low parameters by representing a degree level. Three indicators were included for each of the 17 descriptors (Hord, Meehan, Orletsky, & Sattes, 1999).

A field test was designed to continue to study the reliability or consistency of the instrument. The sample for the field test included a total of 690 teachers representing 21 schools in the mid-east section of the country. The teacher participants represented elementary, middle/junior high, and high schools. Analyses of the instrument included descriptive statistics, reliability analyses (internal consistency and stability or test-retest), and validity analyses (content, concurrent, and construct) (Hord et al., 1999). The field test assessing reliability and validity were satisfactorily met, thus indicating that the 17-item instrument was very useful as a measure of a school's professional staff as a learning community.

Ongoing research on schools as professional learning communities has generated a need for a new PLC assessment that reflects the reconceptualization of the dimensions and attributes of professional learning communities. While Hord's *School Professional Staff as Learning Community* questionnaire (1998) has been successfully utilized as a measure to assess teacher perceptions about the school staff as a learning organization, some misalignment has been noted between responses indicated by staff on the questionnaire and actual observations and interviews within the school setting. This research study has produced evidence indicating a perception by staff of being further along the PLC continuum than the evidence derived through principal and teacher interviews shows. Our reconceptualization of the PLC dimensions, the critical attributes, and the development of the Professional Learning Community Organizer (PLCO) (see figure 2.4) has created a need for a new measure. This new instrument has been developed to more accurately represent the phases of development from initiation to implementation to institutionalization (Fullan, 1985).

PROFESSIONAL LEARNING
COMMUNITY ASSESSMENT

The Professional Learning Community Assessment (PLCA) (see figure 8.1) extends Hord's work and is designed to assess perceptions about the school's principal, staff, and stakeholders (parents and community members) based on the five dimensions of a professional learning community and the critical attributes (Olivier, Hipp, & Huffman, 2003). The questionnaire contains statements about practices that occur at the school level. This measure serves as a more descriptive tool of those practices observed at the school level relating to shared and supportive leadership; shared values and vision; collective learning and application; shared personal practice; and supportive conditions, both relationships and structures.

An initial phase of this study was designed to provide evidence of construct validity for this new measure. A panel of 76 expert educators was chosen to provide data as to the importance of 44 statements about practices occurring at the school level. This Expert Study was conducted in order to determine the importance and relevance of each instrument item.

Directions:

This questionnaire assesses your perceptions about your principal, staff, and stakeholders based on the five dimensions of a professional learning community (PLC) and related attributes. There are no right or wrong responses. This questionnaire contains a number of statements about practices that occur in some schools. Read each statement and then use the scale below to select the scale point that best reflects your personal degree of agreement with the statement. Shade the appropriate oval provided to the right of each statement. Be certain to select only one response for each statement.

Key Terms:

\#   Principal = Principal, not Associate or Assistant Principal

\#   Staff = All adult staff directly associated with curriculum, instruction, and assessment of students

\#   Stakeholders = Parents and community members

Scale: 1 = Strongly Disagree (SD)
            2 = Disagree (D)
            3 = Agree (A)
            4 = Strongly Agree (SA)

STATEMENTS	SCALE			
Shared and Supportive Leadership	SD	D	A	SA
1. The staff are consistently involved in discussing and making decisions about most school issues.	0	0	0	0
2. The principal incorporates advice from staff to make decisions.	0	0	0	0
3. The staff have accessibility to key information.	0	0	0	0
4. The principal is proactive and addresses areas where support is needed.	0	0	0	0
5. Opportunities are provided for staff to initiate change.	0	0	0	0
6. The principal shares responsibility and rewards for innovative actions.	0	0	0	0
7. The principal participates democratically with staff sharing power and authority.	0	0	0	0
8. Leadership is promoted and nurtured among staff.	0	0	0	0
9. Decision making takes place through committees and communication across grade and subject areas.	0	0	0	0
10. Stakeholders assume shared responsibility and accountability for student learning without evidence of imposed power and authority.	0	0	0	0

Figure 8.1. Professional Learning Community Assessment.

	STATEMENTS	SCALE			
	Shared Values and Vision	SD	D	A	SA
11.	A collaborative process exists for developing a shared sense of values among staff.	0	0	0	0
12.	Shared values support norms of behavior that guide decisions about teaching and learning.	0	0	0	0
13.	The staff share visions for school improvement that have an undeviating focus on student learning.	0	0	0	0
14.	Decisions are made in alignment with the school's values and vision.	0	0	0	0
15.	A collaborative process exists for developing a shared vision among staff.	0	0	0	0
16.	School goals focus on student learning beyond test scores and grades.	0	0	0	0
17.	Policies and programs are aligned to the school's vision.	0	0	0	0
18.	Stakeholders are actively involved in creating high expectations that serve to increase student achievement.	0	0	0	0
	Collective Learning and Application	SD	D	A	SA
19.	The staff work together to seek knowledge, skills, and strategies and apply this new learning to their work.	0	0	0	0
20.	Collegial relationships exist among staff that reflect commitment to school improvement efforts.	0	0	0	0
21.	The staff plan and work together to search for solutions to address diverse student needs.	0	0	0	0
22.	A variety of opportunities and structures exist for collective learning through open dialogue.	0	0	0	0
23.	The staff engage in dialogue that reflects a respect for diverse ideas that lead to continued inquiry.	0	0	0	0
24.	Professional development focuses on teaching and learning.	0	0	0	0
25.	School staff and stakeholders learn together and apply new knowledge to solve problems.	0	0	0	0
26.	School staff is committed to programs that enhance learning.	0	0	0	0

Figure 8.1. *(Continued)*

STATEMENTS	SCALE			
Shared Personal Practice	**SD**	**D**	**A**	**SA**
27. Opportunities exist for staff to observe peers and offer encouragement.	0	0	0	0
28. The staff provide feedback to peers related to instructional practices.	0	0	0	0
29. The staff informally share ideas and suggestions for improving student learning.	0	0	0	0
30. The staff collaboratively review student work to share and improve instructional practices.	0	0	0	0
31. Opportunities exist for coaching and mentoring.	0	0	0	0
32. Individuals and teams have the opportunity to apply learning and share the results of their practices.	0	0	0	0
Supportive Conditions—Relationships	**SD**	**D**	**A**	**SA**
33. Caring relationships exist among staff and students that are built on trust and respect.	0	0	0	0
34. A culture of trust and respect exists for taking risks.	0	0	0	0
35. Outstanding achievement is recognized and celebrated regularly in our school.	0	0	0	0
36. School staff and stakeholders exhibit a sustained and unified effort to embed change into the culture of the school.	0	0	0	0
Supportive Conditions—Structures	**SD**	**D**	**A**	**SA**
37. Time is provided to facilitate collaborative work.	0	0	0	0
38. The school schedule promotes collective learning and shared practice.	0	0	0	0
39. Fiscal resources are available for professional development.	0	0	0	0
40. Appropriate technology and instructional materials are available to staff.	0	0	0	0
41. Resource people provide expertise and support for continuous learning.	0	0	0	0
42. The school facility is clean, attractive, and inviting.	0	0	0	0
43. The proximity of grade level and department personnel allows for ease in collaborating with colleagues.	0	0	0	0

Figure 8.1. (*Continued*)

STATEMENTS		SCALE		
44.	Communication systems promote a flow of information among staff.	0 0 0 0		
45.	Communication systems promote a flow of information across the entire school community including: central office personnel, parents, and community members.	0 0 0 0		

Figure 8.1. *(Continued)*

These educators represented various levels of professional practice, including classroom teachers, principals, assistant principals, district and regional administrators, university faculty members, and educational researchers. Each expert was asked to rate (High, Medium, Low) the importance of each practice as an item to be included in an assessment about perceptions of a school as a professional learning community. Ninety-eight percent of the items were rated as High in importance with only one item receiving a rating of Medium in terms of relevance. All 44 items were retained for the initial field test; additionally, one item was divided into two statements for a total of 45 items.

The next phase of the study included a field test of the PLCA instrument in schools. In order to assess perceptions based on the five dimensions of a professional learning community, participants were asked to respond to statements about practices that occur in schools. The PLCA utilized a four-point, forced choice Likert scale ranging from 1 = Strongly Disagree to 4 = Strongly Agree. The field test resulted in 247 completed and usable surveys. Descriptive statistics included minimum and maximum values (1 and 4), item means, and standard deviations. Item #42 (The school facility is clean, attractive, and inviting) resulted in the highest mean score (3.35) and factored in the supportive conditions dimension. Conversely, item #27 (Opportunities exist for staff to observe peers and offer encouragement), within the shared personal practice dimension, yielded the lowest mean score (2.39).

Factor analysis was the method selected to provide evidence of construct validity. The analyses utilized a series of statistical procedures for the total sample of respondents (n = 247). Factor identification consisted of items reflecting the five dimensions of professional learning communities. While selection of the factors resulted from the statistical procedures, a critical choice incorporated the best conceptual and theoretical fit.

Cronbach's Alpha internal consistency reliability coefficients were computed for the factored subscales of the measure. For the five factored subscales, the Alpha coefficients ranged from a low of .83 (Collective Learning and Application and Supportive Conditions–Relationships and Structures) to a high of .93 (Shared Values and Vision). Thus, the instrument yielded satisfactory internal consistency (Alpha coefficient) reliability for the factored subscales.

The Professional Learning Community Assessment instrument is available for dissemination and use by educators and others as an assessment tool that measures practices observed at the school level relating to the five dimensions of a professional learning community and their critical attributes. The results of testing indicate that this instrument is very useful as a measuring tool to assess perceptions based on the five dimensions of a PLC. With continued and expanded use of the PLCA measure, assessing these perceptions as noted by practices within the schools will continue to evolve, thus strengthening the database. This diagnostic tool is intended to support and enhance the development of professional learning communities and contributes to continuous learning and school improvement.

Note: In this chapter, factor analyses used Varimax procedures with principal components and Orthogonal rotations. General decision rules were used to retain items on particular factors.

9

The PLC Connection to School Improvement

D'Ette Fly Cowan

The preceding chapters offer a deeper understanding of each of the five dimensions of professional learning communities (Hord, 1997a) and how educators can assess their schools. Although the dimensions have been discussed individually, studies of schools striving to become professional learning communities have revealed the highly interdependent and interrelated nature of the dimensions. In the real business of school improvement, the dimensions are addressed holistically, simultaneously, and recursively to achieve desired change. Substantial and continuous improvement of schools, like other organizations, requires a context that is conducive to change—one that supports both individuals and the organization as a whole. Schools operating as professional learning communities offer such a context.

A NEW APPROACH TO SCHOOL IMPROVEMENT

Studies of organizational change in the corporate sector (Argyris, 1993; Block, 1993; Deming, 1986; Gardner, 1990; Senge, 1990) laid important groundwork for examining the ways in which schools currently operate and for explaining why so many have limited success in achieving desired results in student learning. Such studies revealed that increasing the capacity of individuals within an organization to grow and learn together enabled the organization as a whole to improve and to overcome seemingly

75

insurmountable challenges. Senge discovered that some organizations used the collective creative talents of everyone to "invent" solutions to their organizations' problems and were more intent on *learning* rather than *controlling*. He described these learning organizations as those in which

> people continually expand their capacity to create the results they truly de-
> sire, where new and expansive patterns of thinking are nurtured, where col-
> lective aspiration is set free, and where people are continually learning how
> to learn together. (p. 3)

Within such organizations, there was no end point, no final destination, no moment when participants could stop and say, "We have arrived; our work is done." Rather, the journey is one of continuous inquiry and improve-
ment—largely because life all around the organization is in a state of change. Participants within these organizations engage in continuous improvement, finding ways to be ever more productive through the knowledge, skill, and commitment of those working within the organization for shared goals.

This understanding contributes significantly to the work of school im-
provement and is aligned with Fullan and Miles' (1992) notion that "change involves learning and . . . all change involves coming to under-
stand and to be good at something new" (p. 749). Increasingly, compelling arguments advocate that schools learn how to re-create themselves into learning organizations to achieve desired outcomes. Change of this sort reaches into the very core of what the school does and how it does it. It assumes strengthening the most basic linkage of vital aspects of school improvement—the *teacher* working with *students* to gain deep knowledge and understanding of *subject matter*. It focuses, first and foremost, upon learning on the part of the professionals in the school as the way to increase learning on the part of students.

Part of the learning that occurs within a learning community helps the staff to make good decisions—to embrace changes that are supported by research and practice and that are feasible under their specific circum-
stances. It also helps them to eschew changes (often in the form of new programs) that have undocumented success for students. It keeps staffs from being distracted by "enthusiastic but short-lived fads" (Lashway, 1998) and focuses on more powerful and lasting efforts that help schools

become systematic, collaborative problem-solving organizations that can continually develop and implement new ideas.

Hargreaves (1995) noted that within schools operating as learning communities, adults review and renew their shared purpose over time; formulate policies that respond to local circumstances and student needs; and alter school cultures of individualism, isolation, and balkanization into cultures of collaboration. These schools reflect a change in traditional relationships among teachers, students, parents, administrators, and community. As stakeholders, individuals within these schools commit to shared organizational learning that balances continuous improvement with heritage, tradition, continuity, and consolidation, and applies positive politics to benefit students.

Leading scholars (Darling-Hammond, 1996; Leithwood, Jantzi, & Steinbach, 1995; Little, 1997; McLaughlin & Talbert, 1993) agree that school improvement of a lasting nature can be accomplished only when school staff members identify the school's unique concerns and then direct their own learning to how to solve their problems. When all teachers in a school engage *intentionally* and *continuously* in the learning process, rather than in isolated pockets and in uncoordinated efforts, the capacity of the school to solve problems and maintain focus and commitment is powerfully enhanced. Hord (1997) noted that staffs that participate in continuous inquiry and improvement of this kind transform themselves into professional learning communities and constantly renew themselves for the important work they do.

PROFESSIONAL LEARNING
COMMUNITY AND SCHOOL IMPROVEMENT

What, then, are the connections between Hord's dimensions of professional learning communities and school improvement? When each dimension is considered separately, numerous connections become apparent.

Shared and Supportive Leadership

The existence of a collegial relationship among principals and teachers is a powerful aspect of creating a professional learning community. Such a relationship provides opportunities for broad-based participation in decisions for school improvement. Principals, rather than serving as the sole decision makers, seek ways to share decision-making authority formally and informally with others and thereby increase the leadership capacity of school staffs. This practice requires, however, that principals relinquish some of their power to allow their staffs to genuinely participate in shared learning and decision making about substantive issues related to student learning (Leithwood, Leonard, & Sharratt, 1997).

In places where decision making is broadly shared, teachers no longer merely serve as implementers of change envisioned by someone far removed from the classroom and students. Instead, teachers, along with their fellow staff, help to create the vision, identify changes that are needed to attain the vision, and then decide how these changes are to be implemented and monitored. Prestine (1993) noted that in learning communities, the role of principals as primary decision makers becomes reconceptualized to one in which they share authority, facilitate the work of staff, and participate without dominating. Klein-Kracht (1993) suggested that these reconceptualized roles require administrators to work *along with* teachers in the quest for effective solutions to school problems.

> The traditional pattern that "teachers teach, students learn, and administrators manage is completely altered. . . . [There is] no longer a hierarchy of who knows more than someone else, but rather the need for everyone to contribute. (p. 393)

Shared Values and Vision

In the work of school improvement, shared values and a common vision help to focus the school staff on the work to be accomplished. Staffs organized as professional learning communities operate from a set of commonly acknowledged values that contribute to a shared vision of who they are and the work they do. Hord (1997) noted that "a core characteristic of the professional learning community is an undeviating focus on student learning" (p. 13).

Shared values and vision serve a particular purpose in binding the norms of behavior within a school. Such norms are manifested in shared responsibility for student learning, a caring environment, open communication, a balance of personal and common ambition, and trusting relationships. Newmann (cited in Brandt, 1995) asserted that this concerted group effort, grounded in shared values and vision for ultimate outcomes, pushes for learning of high intellectual quality on the part of both students and school professionals. Furthermore, a high expectation for learning exists for *all* students regardless of gender, ethnicity, or economic background.

Collective Learning and Application

In schools where the staff is functioning as a learning community, multiple constituencies (e.g., teachers, paraprofessionals, parents, community representatives, and students) collaborate to develop desired characteristics in their school. The collaboration to achieve shared goals becomes focused, intentional, and urgent. Participants look both outward and inward to find answers to their problems, studying what can be learned from the larger research community and conducting self-examination of root causes below the surface in their own school contexts.

Collaborators plan, identify, and implement innovative approaches to solve problems using the enhanced creative capacity wrought by discussion and dialogue on critical issues about students, teaching, and learning. Griffin (cited in Sergiovanni, 1994) believed that employing such an inquiry process to address problems has multiple benefits in fostering a sense of community among principals and teachers.

> As principals and teachers inquire together, they create community. Inquiry helps them to overcome chasms caused by various specializations of grade level and subject matter. Inquiry forces debate among teachers about what is important. Inquiry promotes understanding and appreciation for the work of others. . . . And inquiry helps principals and teachers create the ties that bind them together as a special group and that bind them to a shared set of ideas. Inquiry, in other words, helps principals and teachers become a community of learners. (p. 154)

Morrissey (2000) notes that schools engaging in inquiry about substantive issues "move beyond discussions of revising the schedule or establishing new governance procedures to focus on areas that can contribute to significant school improvement—curriculum, instruction, assessment, and the school's culture" (p. 8). Findings suggest that when a whole faculty identifies an important issue related to student success and work on it together, the relationships needed to sustain the improvement efforts over time are developed in the process.

Shared Personal Practice

Shared personal practice is the key to changing what occurs in the classroom, and this is at the heart of school improvement. A process through which teachers can review their colleagues' behaviors and classroom practices in a facilitative rather than evaluative context is a critical aspect of a professional learning community in breaking down walls of isolation and independent practice (Louis & Kruse, 1995). Elmore (1999/2000) stated,

> Schools and school systems that are improving directly and explicitly confront the issue of isolation by creating multiple avenues of interaction among educators and promoting inquiry-oriented practices while working toward high standards of student performance. (p. 32)

Wignall (1992) found that in a school in which this dimension exists, teachers seek and find help from others and develop warm relationships with one another. This relationship serves as a foundation for examination of classroom practice and sustains teachers in times of adversity and challenge. Teachers tolerate (even encourage) debate, discussion, and disagreement. They are comfortable sharing both their successes and their failures. They praise and recognize one another's triumphs, and offer empathy and support for each other's troubles.

Such interactions, however, can be expected only after mutual respect and trust are achieved among staff members. For that reason, this dimension is relatively rare in all but the most advanced schools in becoming professional learning communities. Nevertheless, the work of school improvement must give attention to creating a culture in which such practice is not simply implemented, but also valued.

Supportive Conditions

Two categories of conditions support schools as professional learning communities as they engage in school improvement (Boyd, 1992; Louis & Kruse, 1995). *Relationships*, one category of supportive conditions, are manifested in positive teacher attitudes toward schooling, students, and change; student interest and engagement in learning; norms of continuous critical inquiry and improvement; and shared vision and purpose (Boyd, 1992). Involvement in decision making, collegial relationships, and positive student-teacher-administrator relationships all contribute to a sense of community in the school improvement process. Relationships are significantly enhanced by a culture of respect and trust among colleagues, appropriate skill and knowledge in teaching and learning, support from administrators, and intensive socialization processes (Hord, 1998).

Structures, a second category of supportive conditions can be redesigned to reduce isolation, provide time for teachers to collaborate, enhance teacher-student interactions, and increase physical proximity of the staff to one another. When designed appropriately, these structures foster interdependent teaching roles, effective communication, teacher empowerment, and a sense of school identity. External factors such as school policies and assistance from central office staff can also be redesigned to promote greater autonomy, increased collaboration, and meaningful professional development opportunities.

While these categories of supportive conditions have been discussed separately herein, in the actual work of school improvement, it is difficult to separate the two. They are, in reality, highly interactive and interdependent, yet key to maintaining the growth and development of a learning community.

CONCLUSION

The connections between professional learning communities and school improvement have become increasingly clear. We should first recognize that the creation of a professional learning community is not an end in itself. It is, rather, an infrastructure for supporting school improvement so that, ultimately, the level and quality of student learning increases. Furthermore, the creation of a professional learning community cannot be prescriptive or expected to follow a linear course. It entails all of the challenges, surprises, and complexities one might expect in addressing core aspects of schooling, including organizational goals and roles, staff needs and skills, and the dynamics of the external and internal contexts. Perhaps most noteworthy, it represents a fundamental change in the way many schools and those associated with them operate, and, for that reason, it is not the type of work for the fainthearted.

Nevertheless, school staffs operating as learning communities have significant potential for positive impact on student learning. Wheatley (1994) described the challenge in helping to improve schools through such a process.

> I believe that we have only just begun the process of discovering and inventing the new organizational forms that will inhabit the twenty-first century. To be responsible inventors and discoverers, though, we need the courage to let go of the old world, to relinquish most of what we cherished, to abandon our interpretations about what does and doesn't work. As Einstein is often quoted as saying: "No problem can be solved from the same consciousness that created it. We must learn to see the world anew." (p. 5)

This chapter provides evidence that school improvement supported within the professional learning community context increases the capacity of school staffs to improve student learning. As an infrastructure that fosters shared leadership, unites a staff behind a common purpose, enhances collaboration, supports teachers in making instructional changes that benefit students, and encourages shared practice, it serves as a credible context for initiating, supporting, and sustaining school improvement.

4

FIVE CASE STUDIES

10

Case Study Overview

It is all the rage for people to say that the latest wave of reform will be the reform that is going to make the difference. . . . Our evidence suggests that even when there seems to be consensus that change is needed and even when dedicated and well-intentioned people are trying to bring it about, issues and problems—often unanticipated—arise that threaten and impede the change process almost from its inception. . . . Many lessons still need to be learned about achieving the ambitious aims of current reform efforts.

> —D. E. Muncey & P. J. McQuillan, "Preliminary
> findings from a five-year study of the Coalition
> of Essential Schools," *Phi Delta Kappan*

Fullan (1995, 2000) added that most school reform efforts have created overload and fragmentation, thereby resulting in a lack of coherence and meaning, which continues to divert us from the issues of greatest importance—teaching and learning. For instance, many governance structures have been designed to empower a greater number of staff in decision making, yet students fail to benefit. Efforts are often unrelated to curriculum and instructional issues, and systems are not aligned to focus on the process it takes to move students to higher levels of achievement (Fullan, 1995; Guskey & Peterson, 1993; Lindle, 1995/1996; Newmann & Wehlage, 1995). In the guise of teacher empowerment, "traditional opportunities for teacher decision-making have done little to advance the professionalism of teachers, or to involve them in critical educational concerns (Brown, 1995, p. 337).

The accounts of these school reform efforts come and go, often carrying rich details of their stories with them. So, how do schools move from concept to capability? How do schools move from norms of isolation to norms of collaboration, inquiry, and community? How do schools grow into mature professional communities? How can school leaders become prepared to create communities that continuously learn and improve teaching and student performance?

The purpose of providing these five case studies for analysis is based on multiple years of working in schools endeavoring to create professional learning communities. Each author was the external change agent at the site described in the case study. The schools include PreK–12 schools in urban, suburban, and rural settings across four states.

The level of readiness of these five schools is based on Fullan's Model of Initiation, Implementation, and Institutionalization, which is most commonly illustrated as "The Implementation Dip" (1990, 1991). These three distinct phases through which an innovation progresses to meet desired outcomes emerged from an extensive review of the literature on change. The five stories are distinguishable along a continuum of change ranging from *initiation* to *implementation*. Two of the case studies are at the initiation level, while the other three schools are viewed as implementing the innovation. None of the cases are at the level of institutionalization. It should be noted that the schools selected for the following case studies include only some of the six high-readiness schools that are the focus of this book in chapters 3 through 7. The stories reflect the following descriptors:

School 1: Elementary, low-income suburban, implementation
School 2: High school, middle-income rural, implementation
School 3: Middle school, middle-income suburban, implementation
School 4: Middle school, middle- to low-income rural, initiation
School 5: Elementary, low-income rural, initiation

The general purpose of these stories is to allow participants to analyze information presented and generate further questions and areas of interest

DIMENSIONS

	Shared and Supportive Leadership	Shared Values and Vision	Collective Learning and Application	Shared Personal Practice	Supportive Conditions
#1 Role Expectations	X				X
#2 Nurturing the Human Side		X			X
#3 Trust as a Foundation		X	X		X
#4 Role of Principal Commitment	X		X		X
#5 Reculturing a School			X	X	X

(Left margin label: **CASE STUDIES**)

Figure 10.1.   Case-study matrix.

in need of study. Each case study illustrates one or more dimensions as displayed in figure 10.1. The stories are presented and include the following sections based on Kowalski's (1995) case study analysis format:

- Background (introductory text in each chapter)
- Key areas of reflection
- The case
- The challenge
- Key questions

We hope readers will challenge each other's thinking with these authentic stories, which reflect multiple and confounding issues. Our primary goal in presenting these case studies is to stimulate inquiry among faculty and students in educational leadership programs, as well as among school administrators and school staff. Moreover, we urge educators to generate their own perspectives, identify related issues and problems, and develop potential solutions or next steps.

11

Case Study #1: Role Expectations in Schools Moving to Site-Based Leadership

Jane Bumpers Huffman

School governance is a complex and usually difficult concept to implement successfully. Generally, schools are guided in this decision by district and state guidelines or mandates. In certain states a site-based managed system is thought to be the best way to administer site business. Each school must have a team or committee that deals with identified issues. This is the situation in the following case study.

Brown (1990) defined school or site-based management as a practice through which a school is allocated money to purchase supplies, equipment, utilities, and other services deemed necessary to meet the needs of the school, including personnel. Yet interpretations of site-based management differ widely. They can be more encompassing than Brown's definition or may be more restrictive as to the amount of empowerment the site is allowed by the central office. Additionally, the extent of shared decision making can be directly influenced by the leadership style of the principal and his or her commitment to site-based management.

Comer (1988) found schools that practiced site-based management, shared decision making, and engaged in ongoing improvement were more likely to be successful because they worked to achieve the following goals:

- Principals who provided instructional leadership
- School climate that was safe
- Positive parent involvement
- Faculty and staff who believed all children can learn

- Reading, writing, and arithmetic as high priorities
- Frequent evaluation of students and staff
- Staff development
- High student attendance
- Students with high expectations of themselves
- Careful planning of special programs

To achieve these goals, the principal must provide outstanding leadership skills. The skills represented can be implemented in many different styles. Getzels, Lipham, and Campbell (1968) defined transactional leadership as leadership that integrates the expectations of the organization with the needs of the people in the organization. This style concentrates on maintaining the status quo and meeting expectations. Leithwood (1992) described transformational leadership as facilitative influence and power that is manifested through other people instead of over other people. This leadership involves collaboration, teacher empowerment, and change. Thus, a critical issue in site-based management is the role the principal plays in leading new change initiatives. Lambert (1998) explained,

> Among the more important tasks for the principal is to establish collegial relationships in an environment that may previously have fostered dependency relationships. It is more difficult to build leadership capacity among colleagues than to tell colleagues what to do. (p. 24)

What is the leadership style that successfully guides the faculty and staff through change? How is that leadership shared with the assistant principal, teacher leaders, and other members of the staff? Katzenmeyer and Moller (1996) viewed the new role of the teacher in this way:

> Teachers can be leaders of change beyond their classrooms by accepting more responsibility for helping colleagues. These leadership roles empower teachers to develop their leadership skills while still focusing on their teaching roles. (p. 7)

The following case study looks at these various stakeholder roles and examines the issues related to the responsibilities of the Campus Leadership Team. Concerns in this case study emerge that deal with trust, respect, communication, decision making, curriculum, and use of time.

KEY AREAS FOR REFLECTION

- The principal's dilemma regarding the traditional view of leadership.
- Faculty involvement and commitment in the Campus Leadership Team.
- The role of the assistant principal in campus leadership and management.
- The concerns and responsibilities of a teacher leader pursuing an administrative career.

THE CASE

Northland Elementary, a K–5 school located in a city with a population of 90,000, is located within 30 miles of two major southern cities. The city has two large universities and serves as a central service center for the northern part of the state. The school was built in 1973 and operates with an alternative calendar that serves students year-round.

The student community is 50% Hispanic, 38% white, 11% African American, and 2% other. Students' families are mostly low-income semi-skilled and unskilled laborers. Most parents have acquired a high school diploma.

In the school there are 42 certified staff, 10 paraprofessionals, and 10 support personnel. Sixteen percent of the staff are male and 84% are female. In the ethnicity category, 61% of the staff are white, 30% are Hispanic, and 9% are African American. Twenty-one percent of the staff members have master's degrees. Twenty-two staff members have 0–10 years teaching experience. Twelve teachers have taught at Northland for more than 11 years, and fifteen teachers are in their first or second year of teaching.

The Principal's Dilemma

When Grayson Dunagan was promoted to principal, he realized many challenges would confront him. The school needed to consider changes that would serve the Hispanic majority students as well as meet the needs of the white and African American students. Initiating programs to increase parent involvement in their children's education had been suggested. Since Grayson had been the assistant principal for several years, he felt confident he knew the school, students, faculty, and staff, and that he could initiate these necessary changes. His traditional leadership style reflected a reliance on rules and regulations. He believed he had to appear in control of the situation and be clear about who was in charge of the decision making.

One of the first major challenges came from the state rather than from student, teacher, or parent concerns. The mandate from the state, which was supported by the district, was that site-based management would begin the following year, and each school must be in compliance.

What did this mean? The primary change would be to move from a transactional leader to a transformational leader in order to institute shared decision making through a Campus Leadership Team (CLT). This team included administrators, teachers, a central office representative, parents, and community representatives. The team's charge was to develop and ratify the Campus Improvement Plan submitted annually to the state and to make other major site decisions related to hiring, curriculum, budget, resource allocation, and other critical issues.

● Grayson was stunned. How would he handle this situation? He knew he must involve all the stakeholders, but wouldn't this erode his ability to determine the best plan for the school and get results for students? After all, aren't the students the most important consideration?

Faculty Involvement

After a faculty meeting where Grayson explained the new campus organization, several teachers began discussing their concerns. "How can we attend one more committee meeting?" Yolanda, a first-grade teacher, wonders. "The principal usually makes the decisions. If we have to represent our grade level at the Campus Leadership Team, it will take away time from the preparation in our classroom. I feel overwhelmed."

Martha, a kindergarten teacher responds, "The CLT members will be involved in all the major decisions. We will be sharing the decision making on goal setting, budgeting, curriculum issues, book adoptions, school renovations, and hiring new faculty. It will take quite a commitment of time, but more people will be involved in our school."

Ed, a third-grade teacher, questions whether this committee would be an elite group that doesn't really represent the teachers. Joy, another kindergarten teacher explains,

> The CLT will meet every other Tuesday afternoon after school. There is a grade-level representative who takes notes and then reports to the grade level the next day in grade-level meetings. Important issues will be discussed by all of us and we will have the opportunity to express our opinions based on the facts. In addition to administrators and teachers, the team will include paraprofessionals, parents, business representatives, and a central office administrator.

"But Mr. Dunagan generally makes the decisions here at Northland," Yolanda continues. "Do you really think he is going to let us make important decisions? I see this committee as a rubber-stamp committee. I respect Mr. Dunagan, but I'm not sure I trust him to involve us in sharing in these decisions. Is this really worth the time and effort?"

What Does the Assistant Principal Do?

Generally, the role of the assistant principal is to support the principal and assist him or her by completing assigned duties and responsibilities. This varies widely from school to school based on the principal's leadership style and the interaction between the principal and assistant principal. In addition to customary management responsibilities, the assistant principal often shares teacher evaluation duties and is directly involved in staff development and teacher support.

In this case, Marion, the assistant principal, works well with Grayson, but feels left out of the loop. She generally is assigned the management duties such as key inventory, textbooks, facility concerns, and discipline issues. She has a good relationship with the teachers, but does not find the time to be involved in their classrooms with the important curricular issues. Yet many days, when Grayson is out of the building for district meetings or professional development, Marion is left alone to take care of school business.

Regarding the change to site-based management as mandated by the state, Grayson has not consulted Marion as to her opinion about this significant school change. Marion, who is getting her master's in school administration, believes in shared decision making and is anxious to learn more about the Campus Leadership Team and how she can be involved.

Teacher Leadership

Heather Holton, a fifth-grade teacher with seven years experience, is concerned that the school is not meeting the needs of the students. An educational administration master's student also working toward her principal's certificate, she is anxious for the principal and faculty to embrace these reform efforts and begin providing more enlightened leadership for Northland Elementary.

Heather, an energetic teacher with exemplary organizational skills, took the lead in a national project that sought to develop professional learning communities in established schools. She, along with Grayson, attended meetings to gain information about the project. With Grayson's assistance, Heather began sharing that information with the faculty and encouraged them to consider additional reforms.

Yet Heather was often frustrated and didn't understand why other teachers couldn't see the benefits of shared leadership, risk taking, and being involved in programs that addressed the real student problems. These programs required a great deal of work, but (if the teachers would just use their time more efficiently) Heather believed they could get amazing results.

Heather sees the move to site-based management as a progressive step and supports the establishment of the Campus Leadership Team. She believes that this may help the school to share information, make better decisions, and create a climate that supports trust, commitment, and effective communication. Heather hopes this will result in focused goals for student improvement and stronger curricular programs.

THE CHALLENGE

How can Grayson lead the faculty and facilitate the Campus Leadership Team in changing to site-based managed decision making?

KEY QUESTIONS

1. The Principal's Dilemma
   - What choices does Grayson Dunagan have?
   - If you were the principal, what would you do to meet the state mandate?
   - What leadership style and strategies would you use to initiate this change? Why?
2. Faculty Involvement
   - What role do individual faculty members have in influencing how decisions are made in the school?
   - What would be the advantages of sharing decision making with multiple stakeholders?
   - What would be the disadvantages of sharing decision making with multiple stakeholders?
3. What Does the Assistant Principal Do?
   - What is the ideal relationship between the principal and the assistant principal in managing and leading the school?
   - What options does Marion have if she believes she should be involved in different duties and responsibilities?
   - What indicators would an assistant principal identify that would convince her it was time to make a change in her school assignment?
4. Teacher Leadership
   - What role should teacher leaders play in the shared leadership of a school?
   - How does the interplay between less experienced teachers and more veteran teachers affect the decisions made and everyday efforts of all teachers?
   - How do teachers and administrators decide what the expectations of time commitment are for teachers?

- When should teachers be compensated for time spent outside the classroom?

SUGGESTED READINGS

Brown, D. (1990). *Decentralization and school-based management.* Bristol, PA: Falmer Press.

Comer, J. (1988). *Quantitative methods for public administration: Techniques and application.* Fort Worth, TX: Harcourt Brace.

Getzels, J. W., Lipham, J., & Campbell, R. (1968). *Educational administration as a social process.* New York: Harper and Row.

Katzenmeyer, M., & Moller, G. (1996). *Awakening the sleeping giant.* Thousand Oaks, CA: Corwin Press.

Lambert, L. (1998). *Building leadership capacity in schools.* Alexandria, VA: Association for Supervision and Curriculum Development.

Leithwood, K. A. (1992). The move towards transformational leadership. *Educational Leadership, 49*(5), 8–12.

12

Case Study #2: Nurturing the Human Side: A Crucial Component for PLCs

Danna Beaty and Anita M. Pankake

With the rapidly changing demands placed on educators, it is difficult to discern what direction change should take. It is the shared vision and goal of educators to provide students with a safe learning environment that meets the varied academic and social needs of all students. Under the traditional design of schools, this goal is doomed to failure. Sergiovanni stated, "What needs to be improved about schools is their culture, the quality of interpersonal relationships, and the nature and quality of learning experiences" (1994, p. 143). This holds true for students and faculty alike. Professional learning communities (PLCs) provide educational professionals with a forum in which educators share ideas, leadership, and learn from and support each other. According to research conducted by Hord and her colleagues (2000), the foundational factors of a PLC are trust, which promotes risk-taking; honest communication; deep commitment to school initiatives; valued teacher input; and a student-centered school culture.

In order for PLCs to be successful, leadership among teachers must be valued and nurtured. There must be a shared sense of leadership, a shared vision, and a feeling of responsibility for the quality of instruction provided in the classroom among teachers and administrators. Katzenmeyer and Moller (1996) defined teacher leaders as individuals who "lead within and beyond the classroom, influence others toward improved educational practice and identify with and contribute to a community of teacher leaders" (p. 6). They further believe that this leadership "develops naturally among professionals who learn, share and address problems together" (p. 12). Supportive conditions for this behavior—both the physical and human—must be present if leadership and learning are to occur.

KEY AREAS FOR REFLECTION

- Processes and consequences of organizational change
- Sustaining professional development gains
- Developing and balancing shared vision that addresses organizational needs and individual needs
- Developing and sustaining teacher leadership
- Supportive conditions for professional learning communities

THE CASE

The Community

Loston is a rural community of about three thousand. Its economy is largely based on agriculture and the coal, oil, and gas industries. The majority of the workers in the area are semi-skilled and laborers; consequently, the number of low socioeconomic families in the area is high. Because of some recreational lakes in the area, Loston has had an increasing population of retirees and part-time "second home" owners from a nearby urban area. Support for school activities in terms of attendance and fund-raisers is generous and widespread. While enjoying the recognition sports bring to the community, there is less enthusiasm in the community for general financial support of the schools, especially regarding new facility needs and the cost of new technologies. Due to the great number of senior citizens and conservative farmers and ranchers, the concern over passing a much-needed bond referendum weighs heavily on the school personnel and Board of Trustees.

The School District

Southern Edge Independent School District (SEISD) is a rural district comprising approximately 1,450 students, which are housed in three schools: an elementary school, a middle school, and a high school. The student population is 88% white, 6.2% Hispanic, 4.6% African American, 0.8% Asian, and 0.4% Native American. These percentages are reflective of the ethnic and racial makeup of the Loston community as well. Thirty-four percent of students enrolled in the district are economically disadvantaged, which qualifies SEISD for Title I funds districtwide. The elementary school facility—the newest in the district—is 20 years old, but still in good condition. The middle school was originally built in the 1940s and has had several additions and renovations throughout the years. The high school, built in the early 1960s, was intended to accommodate 250 students and currently serves approximately 450 students. The district realizes the need for a new facility and anticipates proposing a bond when the elementary school bond is retired.

Leadership at the district level in SEISD has been stable until this last year. The Board of Education members have enjoyed reelection without opposition, and a single superintendent, Stanton Weeks, had guided the district for the last 10 years. It was during Weeks's tenure as superintendent that the current high school principal, Nattie Stewart, was hired. Nattie, in turn, had selected Cash Holden—former Athletic Director and head football coach—as her assistant principal. In July of 2000, Stanton Weeks retired as superintendent for SEISD and Dexter Turnan assumed that role. Both the superintendency and the Loston community were new to Turnan.

The School

The Southern Edge High School (SEHS) facility is poor at best. The roof leaks continually. The old sewage pipes rupture periodically, spilling waste into the student restrooms and into the hallways. All wiring that has been done for technology purposes can be seen as running exposed conduit along the ceiling and down the classroom walls. Portable buildings surround the main structure in order to provide some needed relief for overcrowded classrooms. Yet the teachers and students here excel in teaching and learning, as evidenced over the past several years based on the state's accountability ratings. For four or five years, SEHS received a high ranking, Recognized, and for the last two years, the school has received the highest rating, Exemplary. However, this was not always the case.

Ten years ago, the high school was rated Low Performing and had a very high teacher and administrator turnover rate—seven principals in six years. With leadership from an outstanding principal, the faculty and staff of SEHS worked to bring their academic program from the brink of disaster to a point of success and pride for the students and community. Through the implementation of innovative practices such as academic teaming, block scheduling, and collaborative instruction and thematic learning, the faculty saw student achievement increase dramatically. They attribute much of this success to their willingness to share a common vision and to take risks. Consequently, when the Southwest Educational Development Laboratory's (SEDL) Co-Developer approached the faculty about participating in the development of a PLC, most staff welcomed the opportunity. Nattie Stewart, the current principal, and the Co-Developer established a faculty steering committee to help initiate the PLC project. After exploring several options, the staff decided to select "Technology" as the focus for the PLC project. It was an area that all faculty members believed they needed to learn more about and also an area that would have a large impact on student learning—to say nothing of the impact on their own learning!

Celebration Day: Reflections and Anticipation

It is a warm spring day and Hope Tchrnowski, the district librarian and high school technology coordinator, anxiously awaits the beginning of the staff development session. Today is the culmination of two years of hard work and perseverance. The faculty has prepared a show-and-tell day so that teachers might highlight the innovative ways they are incorporating technology in their classrooms. The faculty has extended special invitations to the superintendent and to the SEDL representative for the school. For Hope, this day symbolizes great beginnings and an end. This will be the last staff development time that Hope will share with her colleagues as she has decided to leave SEISD for other career opportunities. As exciting as this is, Hope knows she will miss many of the relationships she has formed with her fellow educators and is somewhat concerned about what will happen with some of the staff members she is leaving behind.

To accommodate the staff development event, SEHS students were dismissed early—before lunch. Principal Nattie Stewart and her assistant,

Cash Holden, have been busy taking care of those last-minute office duties while the staff has enjoyed a rare opportunity for an off-campus lunch. As the scheduled hour approaches, Hope is making a final sweep of the hallway to be sure that everyone is ready to begin when she notices Dexter Turnan, the new superintendent, walking up the front steps. Hope had great expectations of Turnan when he took the job of superintendent a little over a year ago. He replaced the retiring superintendent, Stanton Weeks—a man who referred to computers as gadgets and nothing more than another passing educational fad—with the promise of technology expertise and a grand plan for districtwide technology advancement. Turnan touted a background steeped in technology; however, as Hope visited with Turnan throughout the year, she had grown concerned about the true breadth and depth of his actual knowledge. If anything, Turnan had resisted several attempts of the PLC to involve him in the technology-focused endeavor. Hope was both surprised and pleased to see him in attendance today.

Tom Wilkins, the department head for Special Education, was going over something with one of his students at the Circulation Desk. Tom and his student were going to be demonstrating a "smart pen," recently purchased by the department, that would aid students in pronouncing unfamiliar words in the selected reading. Hope remembered Tom and his fellow department members' initial skepticism about participation in the PLC project. Historically, Special Education had been included in schoolwide projects only in minor roles and provided with virtually no resources with which to accomplish the established goals. The Student Support Lab, which had for many years been the only place where students had access to computers, had become outdated and no longer provided students with useful software programs. When technology was selected as the focus for the project, Tom had come to Hope in frustration and despair. Together Hope and Tom created a proposal for new computers, software, and printers that would provide the students served by Tom's department with access to the same resources as students in the mainstream classroom. Hope presented the proposal to the Curriculum Director and was granted permission to order and install the new equipment. Tom and his staff had taken it from there, providing their students with new avenues for learning and the staff with enthusiasm for new teaching approaches.

Along the north wall of the library, Hope noticed the student slide shows being showcased by the foreign language teachers, Cindy and

Patty. Cindy is no stranger to innovative teaching practices and collaborative learning environments—both in her own classroom and as a staff development tool. Cindy has been with the district for many years and has
been a strong leader in the school's movement toward teaming, block
scheduling, collaborative learning, and other endeavors. She is a current
member of the Steering Committee for the PLC project. Today's presentation is a fine example of the excellent teaching that can occur in Cindy's
classroom.

The English team is up next and the group begins to migrate toward the
Title I Lab. This computer lab, although initially a source of tension between Hope and Turnan over tech specifications and design, has been a
blessing for the faculty, staff, and students of SEHS. This is the only place
in the school where an entire class can access computers, printers, scan-
ners, and the Internet at the same time. Teachers have been able to rewrite
instructional lessons, which allows them to focus more on the students' interest in technology. The lab stays booked and students ask to use it before and after school. When the project began, a lab of this sort was the
greatest desire of the faculty. Nattie and Hope worked very hard to come
up with the necessary funding for such an endeavor. Finally, it was decided the Title I money that the school was to receive for the year would
be best utilized by providing students with such a lab. Due to the flexible
scheduling of the lab before, after, and during school hours, all students
would have access to technology that many—if not most—did not have
access to at home. Of all the work that Hope had done with technology at
SEHS, she was the most pleased with this lab.

The English team at SEHS is a close group of three women (Merry,
Holley, and Anna) and one man (Peter, the department head). Holley, the
sophomore English teacher primarily responsible for preparing students
for the writing portion of the state standardized test, is new to the district
and to high school this year. Her background is in elementary and special
education. Holley has done a great job of preparing the students for the
state standardized test this year. Today she is demonstrating the software
program used by the English department to pinpoint the strengths and
weaknesses of students' grammar skills in order to help them prepare for
the test and for future writing experiences.

When Holley approached her early in the school year with an interest
in library science, Hope recognized the opportunity to encourage Holley's

professional development as well as being able to secure an energetic, pleasant replacement for herself. Throughout the year, Hope had worked closely with Holley to familiarize her with the budgeting and operating procedures of the district's three libraries. Clearly, Holley's background in children's literature would be a great asset to the district's library program. When Hope decided to resign, she was pleased that Nattie also saw the strengths that Holley would bring to the job and selected her as the new librarian. Hope could feel good about that aspect of her job; it was the technology piece that concerned her.

The technology component of Hope's job had been difficult at best. She had limited resources to work with and received no compensation for her additional duties. In fact, she had at one point grown so weary of the headaches associated with the job that she told Nattie she could no longer be responsible for the technology. After all, it was not really a part of her job. The responsibility had fallen to her because she had been the only person with the knowledge of the hardware and software. In the end, Hope had abandoned her vow not to handle the technology because central office seemed not to care and it was the students and teachers who were suffering for it. Instead, she had recruited a few of the teachers and trained them to help troubleshoot and peer-teach technology skills in their team meetings.

Sara Trigg, one of the math teachers, had been of particular help to Hope. Sara, like Cindy, had been teaching at SEHS for many years and had been instrumental in the implementation and success of reform initiatives employed by the school. However, during the past several years Sara has been repeatedly wounded by the administration, which viewed her involvement as a photographer and contributing editor for a local newspaper as a conflict of interest. Sara's resulting distrust of the administration and her desire to avoid conflict had caused her to retreat into the safe environment of her classroom. Hope saw this as a great loss for faculty and students, as Sara is one of the most gifted, caring, and talented teachers in the school. Sara's love of technology provided Hope with the opportunity to solicit Sara's help in running the lab. Hope spoke with Nattie about granting Sara a release period every day so that she could coordinate the lab schedule, search for instructional Internet sites for teachers, troubleshoot the technical difficulties, and train students and teachers on the operation of lab equipment and software. This arrangement had provided Hope with some much-needed relief and Sara with the self-esteem booster necessary to begin healing some of the earlier hurt. Hope was very concerned that Sara might be the one who would become responsible for all the technology duties.

Sara was very capable of many of the aspects of the technology position; however, she had only very brief network training that Hope had provided for use in case the network went down when she was absent. Given the district's history, Hope had great doubts as to the central office's willingness to provide Sara with the necessary formal network training. Additionally, Hope knew that the increased responsibilities would take away from preparation and instructional time with students. As Sara's commitment to her students has always been first priority, Hope was concerned that Sara might not be as happy with the added responsibilities. Watching Sara as she enthusiastically stood before her peers engaging them in an interactive algebra lesson she had developed using PowerPoint, a graphing calculator, and an Internet website, Hope could only wonder if Sara would retain her rediscovered love of collaboration and leadership responsibilities in the year ahead.

As the faculty rose for a short break and to relocate to the Vocational-Agriculture shop, Hope's attention was drawn to the bubbly sound of Loren Anders's voice. Loren was a first-year teacher, yet her teaching style, her dedication to her work, and her enthusiasm for change assured Hope that Loren was a great educator with tremendous leadership potential. Students and faculty alike enjoyed her bright spirit and benefited from her willingness to share her technology expertise. She had created curriculum units for her classes and the department using PowerPoint and then made them available online for students who were absent or behind in class. Hope smiled as she watched Loren and Sara head toward the Ag shop together; perhaps they could share some of the technology responsibilities—maybe Hope would suggest this pairing to Nattie. Nattie was really wonderful about listening to and acting on many of Hope's ideas. This suggestion could really be important if the enthusiasm for technology that she was seeing today was to continue to grow the following school year.

The final presentation of the day was being given in the library by the principal and assistant principal, Nattie Stewart and Cash Holden, respectively. Hope listened with the rest of the faculty as Nattie and Cash outlined the new curriculum requirements and course offerings for the upcoming year. They had given this same presentation to Board members and parents three nights before. The presentation was very professional and well executed. The rationale presented for the changes in curriculum was sound and technology seemed to be the link that tied it all together. The plan would likely be implemented with little difficulty by the faculty. However, it concerned Hope that the faculty had had minimal input as to the changes that were to be made. Certainly there had been a meeting of department heads to discuss possible changes, but the tone of the meeting was more, "This is what we want to see; tell us how you can make it work," rather than, "Here is what we are thinking. What are your ideas?" Hope viewed this need for a curriculum change as the perfect challenge for a professional learning community. She could only hope that Nattie and Cash would realize the importance of the faculty developing a shared vision in this new curriculum effort.

Overall, it had been a very productive and successful day. The faculty had much to celebrate and about which to be proud. The knowledge level of the faculty with regard to technology had increased dramatically, and consequently, student use of technology as a learning tool had increased as well. However, Hope was concerned about the apparent decline in shared vision and values between faculty and administration. The strength of SEHS over the last decade had been its individual faculty working collectively for the benefit of the students. It seemed to Hope that so many changes in faculty could really upset the collaborative environment that had served the school so well for so many years.

Would the supportive conditions necessary for the development of teacher leadership and the continuance of the PLC change with these staff changes? Can Nattie and Cash make sure that supportive conditions are there for the people accepting these new responsibilities? Is the school collectively developing a vision, merely undergoing changes as it continues to improve, or declining as a result of these changes? The important question remains, What happens next and who will carry it forward?

THE CHALLENGE

Analyze the administrative behaviors in this case. What do you believe should be done to continue the development of a PLC at Southern Edge High School?

KEY QUESTIONS

1. Are there any common themes or patterns as to why staff changes are occurring at SEHS? If so, what are they?
2. Are there supportive conditions in place for sustaining the development of a PLC at the school? If so, what are they? Do you see the supportive conditions strengthening or weakening with the current staff changes?
3. How would you describe the leadership styles of the high school principal, the assistant principal, and the superintendent in SEISD?
4. Do you see any evidence of teacher leadership at SEHS? If yes, who is involved? What are they doing? What supportive conditions helped these teacher leaders to develop?
5. Are the staff changes in this case unusual in number and influence or are these "normal"? Explain how you came to this conclusion.
6. What role has professional development played in the success of SEHS? Was this professional development effective? Why or why not?
7. Do the administrators in SEISD generally, and those in SEHS particularly, try to address individual needs of personnel as well as the vision and goals of the organization? Is there a balance maintained between these two dimensions? Why or why not? What evidence do you have for your conclusion?
8. Was SEHS a professional learning community? Is it now? Will it be in the next two to four years? Explain your assessments.

SUGGESTED READINGS

Deal, T. E., & Kennedy, A. A. (1982). *Corporate cultures.* Cambridge, MA: Addison-Wesley.

Fullan, M. (2001). *The new meaning of educational change* (3rd ed.). New York: Teachers College Press.

Hord, S. (1997). *Professional learning communities: Communities of continuous inquiry and improvement.* Austin, TX: Southwest Educational Development Laboratory.

Hord, S., Chapman, R., Hinson, R. G., Hipp, K. A., Jacoby, C. L., Huffman, J. B., Pankake, A. M., Sattes, B., Thomas, J. J., & Westbrook, J. (2000). *Multiple mirrors: Reflections on the creation of professional learning communities.* Austin, TX: Southwest Educational Development Laboratory.

Katzenmeyer, M., & Moller, G. (1996). *Awakening the sleeping giant.* Thousand Oaks, CA: Corwin Press.

Sergiovanni, T. J. (1994). *Building community in schools.* San Francisco: Jossey-Bass.

Smith, W. F., & Andrews, R. L. (1989). *Instructional leadership: How principals make a difference.* Alexandria, VA: Association for Supervision and Curriculum Development.

13

Case Study #3: Trust as a Foundation in Building a Learning Community

Kristine Kiefer Hipp

No one can argue the critical role that trust plays in promoting risk-taking, innovation, and experimentation; healthy, collaborative relationships; and organizational cultures essential to school effectiveness (Smith, Hoy, & Sweetland, 2001; Tarter, Sabo, & Hoy, 1995). Trust in schools is built on a foundation of ethical behavior evidenced through empowerment, open dialogue, respect for diverse thought, shared visions and values, and professional practices that recognize the value of all who touch the lives of students. Commitment to student learning and loyalty among staff demand a level of trust where "the exercise of professional judgment rests on the teachers' conviction that they can depend upon each other and the principal even in difficult situations" (Hoy & Hannum, 1997, p. 48). Trust is either present or absent, high or low (Argyris, 1990).

> Low trust has no ending; it can always become lower. The irony is that to deal with that issue by covering it up activates the downward spiral. High trust also has no ending. It feeds on itself and increases and expands. In order for this expansion to occur, however, the issue of trust has to be dealt with openly and competently. Most individuals bypass it. (p. 111)

In middle schools, where students are developmentally "caught in the middle" of childhood and adulthood, team structures, interdisciplinary methods, heterogeneous groups, and differing philosophies require teachers to work interdependently rather than in isolation. The frequency, intensity, and effectiveness of their interactions require trust and open, honest communication. In studying the relationship of organizational health and student achievement in middle schools, Hoy and Hannum (1997) cited Parson's three levels of control that must remain in harmony to meet the most basic needs of students: the technical, the managerial, and the institutional levels.

The *technical level* focuses on academic emphasis evidenced through high expectations, an orderly learning environment, and strong teacher affiliation to the school and each other, and a commitment to the belief that all students can learn. The *managerial level* requires principal behavior that is open, supportive, and guided by norms of equality. Principals hold themselves and their staffs accountable and are influential with superiors to gain support and resources as needed. The *institutional level* reflects the degree to which the school copes with the external environment to maintain the integrity of its staff and programs.

The following case study focuses on a middle school in the Midwest that has been involved with a national project over the past three years in trying to create a professional learning community. The story and challenges that emerge are not based on a single incident, but instead portray the ebb and flow of trust that establishes a rhythm typical of school improvement efforts over time. As you read this case, try to understand the detrimental effects of allowing unattended feelings to fester and grow, ignoring voice, betrayal, and perceptions of favoritism. Try to understand the effects of mistrust on risk, relationships, organizational health, and openness to change, all common challenges faced by the newly assigned principal, Leo Dunn.

KEY AREAS OF REFLECTION

- Trust
- Organizational health
- Reading and shaping culture
- Unresolved conflict

THE CASE

Foxdale Middle School is a state-of-the-art school located in a middle-income suburban district in the Midwest. The school serves 550 African American (19%), Asian (5%), Hispanic (1%), Native American (<1%), and white (75.5%) students in grades 5–8. Twelve percent of these students are defined as economically disadvantaged based on their participation in the free or reduced lunch program. Ten percent of the students are bused from outside the school attendance area. Ten percent of the students are enrolled in special education programs for those with physical, mental, emotional, and learning disabilities. The dominant home language is English, except for three students whose family members communicate through Russian, Urdu, and Taiwanese. Approximately 40% of the parents are professionals, 20% hold technical positions, and 40% hold skilled or semi-skilled labor jobs.

There are 51 professional staff members at Foxdale—30 females and 21 males, predominantly European American. The school has a highly educated, committed faculty with 82% of its teachers having master's degrees. Many are described as "seasoned," with 37 teachers having more than 15 years experience, 11 with 6 to 15 years experience, and only three teachers with less than five years of experience. The attendance rate for students is approximately 95%. Student dropouts are nonexistent, yet a significant number of behavioral referrals occur each year.

Introducing the PLC Project

Approximately five years ago, the Mill Street School District experienced significant restructuring due to declining enrollment and financial restrictions. The community had just voted down a second referendum and the staff felt betrayed having given so much back to students and the community. Morale continued to drop with the new configuration of schools (K, 1–4, 5–8) and the mounting pressure to provide an exemplary education to students who fed into the most competitive high school in the state. Long-standing teams at Foxdale were divided, and incoming staff expressed varying philosophies about students, teaching, and learning. As some staff worked to build effective teams, other teams were closed and competitive, reflecting a "your kids v. our kids" mentality.

Rebecca Johnston, once a parent of children at Foxdale and a past member of the school board, was completing her first year as principal. She exhibited a significantly different leadership style than the past two principals. Rebecca had a reputation as a change agent and was committed to changing the climate, the image, and the achievement levels of the students. Her approach was perceived as tough, top-down, and unalterably committed to student learning. At the end of her first year, she was presented an opportunity to become a part of the Southwest Educational Development Laboratory (SEDL) project, a federal project that focused on creating professional learning communities (PLCs).

Rebecca wasted no time in meeting with the superintendent, Paul Kingsman, to share information and gather his impressions. He considered the opportunity intriguing, congruent with the school district's vision, and wholeheartedly supported the effort despite two potential barriers that could hinder participation. First, the significant educational experience of staff might cause skepticism about "another" school reform effort. Second, many teachers would be retiring over the next five to seven years, and he wondered how open they would be to what could be perceived as another initiative at this time in their careers. Not to be discouraged, Rebecca scheduled a series of meetings beginning with the school's Leadership Team to allow the Co-Developer to share the project. The overview of the SEDL project stimulated enthusiasm and hope for change amid a climate of distrust that had evolved from a growing lack of confidence from parents and community members. Rather quickly, the Leadership Team developed a strategy to introduce the project at the next staff meeting.

Bucky Masters, the head union negotiator and an influential member of the leadership team, assisted the Co-Developer in presenting the project at an all-school faculty meeting. Toward the end of the presentation, he asked the staff, "Are you satisfied with the way things are in the school and district, and if not, are you open to try[ing] something new?" The staff discussed issues of morale and raised two major concerns: Would the project add one more thing to their already full agenda? Could time be restructured for the dialogue necessary to learn and share collectively? It was explained that the project would not be an add-on, but would help to integrate current school initiatives. It was quickly apparent that integration and alignment of efforts were imperative. It was also believed by veteran staff that the project would recapture the caring sense of family that was highly evident under the previous principal.

In order to address the issue of time, which was critical to the success of this effort, Bucky and Rebecca developed a plan to add time to the school day in order to gain two "banking days" for professional development. Since this decision had districtwide implications, they proposed adjusting the teacher contract by adding five minutes to each school day to, in turn, gain four half-days, spread throughout the year, for professional development. This adjustment was not a final solution to the problem, but if Bucky and Rebecca could gain support for the plan by teachers, administrators, and school board members, this could turn the tide on trust.

Prior to the start of the school year and the project, the Leadership Team met at Rebecca's lake house to delve deeper into the concept of a learning community, the culture they had committed to create. The team constructed their own meaning of a PLC, through metaphors and on to practical images that could meet the needs of staff and students. Moved by the experience, the team discussed how to replicate the day's activities with all staff to generate the enthusiasm and commitment that they all shared.

Negotiating Time

Since significant time would be needed for teachers to engage in collaborative learning and sharing of practice, certain structures required change. This seemingly small alteration of the school day would affect busing, students, parents, and teachers in three schools. Bucky submitted a formal proposal to the teachers' union for the banking days to engage Foxdale's staff in meaningful activities and dialogue around issues related to student learning. Since the other two schools in this K–8 district were not involved in the project, the vote of confidence required trust and belief in those advocating the change.

A compromise was made that teachers would design half of the professional days while the district administrator would drive the remaining half. An agreement was made in good faith. Next, the issue of transportation was resolved, and the school board approved the proposal. Encouraged by both district and teacher support, Bucky maintained that "the most important step forward was in showing the trust building that we really needed to get going for the staff, because trust is the first level at getting to a PLC."

Just before Thanksgiving, the faculty enjoyed their first banked day preceded by a social the night before. Rebecca attributed the success of the banked time to the team leaders who designed the activities with input from all. On the first evening, a comfortable rustic setting was provided that promoted relationships, as participants shared talents, took risks, and enjoyed engaging in a spirited variety of activities. The next morning, Bucky and a group of male staff members took over the kitchen at Foxdale, preparing a pancake breakfast that would lead to a team-building exercise around relevant issues. The first banked day proved a success, and similar trust-building activities were integrated into events throughout the year.

Reconfiguring the Teams

Now that the banking days were implemented, the school received a long-awaited $92,000 At-Risk grant. Two staff members volunteered to head up an Alternative Program that would begin the next year. Time was of the essence, and Rebecca sought input and support for all members on staff. Besides firming up the design of the program, teams would once again be reconfigured. Three-person teams would become five-person teams and some teachers would shift grades and subject areas. Pupil-teacher ratios would also increase. Apprehension and self-doubt rose, as all staff was not sold on the changing structure. Some staff resorted to indirect means of communication, such as calling school board members with their concerns. Nonetheless, the need for improved programming for at-risk students had been identified as the top priority from a needs assessment conducted two years prior and Foxdale finally had its grant. Hearing of the discontent, Rebecca arranged time for people to express their concerns and work to resolve them. By learning about the nature of change and dealing with opposition compassionately, the wheels were set in motion.

A Return to Standards

Once the Alternative Program was underway and signs of success materialized, the Standards Project again took center stage. The focus on PLC hovered like an "umbrella" over all of the seemingly disconnected initiatives currently in place. A long-range plan had been developed that required core subject area teachers to align their instructional practices and curricular units with locally established teaching standards and benchmarks. Moreover, the district had been working with the Mid-Continent Research for Education and Learning (MCREL), a sister laboratory to SEDL, to establish standards and benchmarks that were aligned with those at the state level.

Rebecca committed one of the two staff meetings per month and every banked day for unit writing within teams and working to connect instructional units to the teaching standards and benchmarks. In addition, Richard Whyte, Foxdale's curriculum specialist, conducted a Standards Academy, which involved a series of optional workshops scheduled on staff inservice days. These sessions were aimed at teachers in the core area subjects to increase applications of critical reasoning skills and knowledge construction strategies. The Standards Academy was an attempt to prepare and allow staff at varying skill levels to create successful interdisciplinary units informed by best practices. A significant amount of support was given to core area teachers, thus some non-core area teachers saw themselves as out of the loop. For instance, financial compensation was provided to the core area teachers for unit writing in the summer—areas that were targeted within the Standards plan. This begged the question, Are some subject areas valued more than others? Moreover, the team-building activities from the previous years were taking a back seat to the Standards effort. Staff missed these events and wanted a greater balance between task- and people-centered activities that included everyone.

Transition

The start of the fourth year brought unexpected change. Richard—the heart, head, and hands of the organization—retired and Rebecca shocked the district by turning in her resignation. The overall effect of these transitions will only become apparent through time, yet pose a challenge for the new principal, Leo Dunn, who must work with unresolved issues.

Nonetheless, Leo has quickly endeared himself to the entire school community. He projects a human side that has been missed and is different from what some perceive as Rebecca's task-oriented style. He is reading the culture, slowing the pace, and working to restore trust. He has provided relief to some teachers, something Rebecca could not do, due to her unwavering focus on student results. Even though she knew that the pace was taking its toll on staff, she failed to understand the diminishing results of such pressure on some staff members.

Issues of Trust

Leo faced teacher-to-principal, teacher-to-teacher, teacher-to-community, and teacher-to-district challenges. The following issues have been identified both through formal interviews and informal conversations. They pose significant problems, as trust is the foundation for building and sustaining a professional learning community.

As the past principal, Rebecca's greatest virtue was possibly her greatest curse—she was unrelentingly goal-oriented and unwavering in her commitment to meeting the needs of students. Despite many accolades among staff and her strong commitment to student learning, pockets of distrust were apparent. A probationary teacher commented, "Some teachers feel an inordinate amount of pressure to achieve without support. I am a probationary teacher and feel debilitated, helpless in a way, like I can't do anything right. I love the students and faculty here, but fear for my job." A veteran staff member revealed, "Rebecca has a tendency to pick out people that she prefers more than others and that has caused hurt. These issues need to be resolved face-to-face."

As in many schools, some teams function better than others. There exist team issues at Foxdale where long-term wounds interfere with healing from the past. There are pockets of distrust and lingering unresolved conflict. Patterns persist and some people find it difficult to forgive and forget. One teacher complained of the "nit-picking" bunch: "I don't like to be a part of them, because their negative energy pulls me down. I don't need anything to pull me down when I'm working so hard. About a third of the people here aren't afraid to try new things and present to the staff. Others do an excellent job in the classroom, but won't come out and share." Another teacher described the essence of an effective team, then portrayed issues at Foxdale. "If the teams don't gel they don't really share beyond a surface level. Even though they are together in space, they are separate. Some teachers had been on the same team for a number of years and that's why it was so hard when their teams were broken up." As a veteran teacher reminisced about the past,

> We were a little nervous about changing teams when we had bonded so well. Our values of teaching and discipline were so similar that we didn't even have to have team meetings that often, things just worked. Other teams were loosey-goosey and that's not handled well by those of us who are more structured and organized. Some people prefer to work in isolation and others get stuck doing all the work. One teacher should just quit because he doesn't really want to be here anymore anyway and another is a walking time bomb. A few people can really hinder openness and trust, which in turn, really hurts the students.

Another example involved two teachers on one team in conflict with one another who had blow-ups in front of students. "One person on the team is nonconfrontational and simply moves inward, while another retreats from the group because he doesn't want to be infected. It affects the whole culture." Two other teachers alluded to the lack of "honest conversation" amid a predominantly close-knit, caring group of teachers. "Staff still shy away from these conversations."

With regard to the external community, the staff still has difficulty getting past two failed referendums. They feel betrayed, as in the words of this teacher who commended the local newspapers, yet contended,

> The community has been afraid of Foxdale, because it looks different, because of the open environment. When I moved here I heard horrible things about how the kids run all over the place, there are no walls, that it's wild. That's a myth that started someplace, so that's the impression around the community. I just want people to talk to our graduates and see the top science winners at the high school who were all from Foxdale. Who were over half of their national merit scholars? Our kids! It's so hard to get past the impressions and let them know what we really have here.

Another teacher concurred, "Community support is not where it should be. We give so much and are committed to doing the best we can. We could be in a situation today where the morale of staff could be devastatingly low, and yet I don't sense that for most of my colleagues. It's a fun place to be and a fun place to work." And yet another commented,

It's a shame because some are not totally comfortable in their neighbor-
hoods discussing what's going on in school. When they are approached by
the opposition, or beat down, it tends to silence them. I think back vividly
to that time when some of the people that I thought in my neighborhood
were really supportive of what I did, and my career, then to have them come
out and take a direct stand against it was a shock, a real disappointment.

Breaking the Agreement

As previously mentioned, the banked days were implemented with an
agreement among all parties: the school board, the administration, and
the teachers' union. Bucky has revealed that "negotiations are holding the
banked days hostage for the next teachers' contract. Our good-faith
agreement has been broken because it was mishandled by the administration in other buildings." Some schools have not allowed joint planning
or teachers working together to design half of the banking days as prom-
ised in the original decision. Since Foxdale was the only school of three
in the district to honor the agreement, the staff are now in jeopardy of los-
ing their banking days, thus the time necessary to promote a professional
learning community. As Bucky states, "This is a huge issue of abuse as
the administrators are only recognizing *their* rights, whereas they have
abused the management of their rights."

THE CHALLENGE

Based on the tenor of the district and existing pockets of distrust at Foxdale, how does Leo Dunn proceed in establishing a sense of trust necessary to continue to build and sustain a learning community?

KEY QUESTIONS

1. How do you get teams to work collaboratively where norms of isolation exist?
2. How do you develop trust amid past wounds—teacher to teacher
   and teacher to administrator?

3. What mechanisms typically exist in middle schools that can be built on to promote a culture of trust?
4. How do you build a sense of inclusiveness, an equal value of all staff members?
5. How do you empower staff to arrive at consensus decision making that is sensitive to *all* staff and students?
6. How do you deal with difficult people so they can work out personal issues themselves?
7. Analyze this case through the lens of Parson's technical, managerial, and institutional levels of control.
8. How should Leo address Argyris's concept of low trust among a few while continuing to build high trust among the many staff members who are committed to building a community of learners that supports student learning?
9. What can Leo do about the banking days?
10. Is the real issue trust?

SUGGESTED READINGS

Argyris, C. (1990). *Overcoming organizational defenses: Facilitating organizational learning.* Upper Saddle River, NJ: Prentice Hall.

Bies, R. J., & Tripp, T. M. (1996). Beyond distrust: "Getting even" and the need for revenge. In R. Kramer & T. Tyler (Eds.), *Trust in Organizations.* Thousand Oaks, CA: Sage.

Blumberg, A., Greenfield, W. D., & Nason, D. (1978). The substance of trust between teachers and principals. *NASSP Bulletin, 62*(9), 76–88.

Evans, K. M. (1993). *Trust and shared governance of schools: A qualitative approach.* Dissertation Abstracts International, *A53/09,* 3059.

Hoy, W. K., & Hannum, J. W. (1997). Middle school climate: an empirical assessment of organizational health and student achievement. *Educational Administration Quarterly, 33*(3), 290–311.

Hoy, W. K., Hannum, J. W., & Tschannen-Moran, M. (1998). Organizational climate and student achievement: A parsimonious view. *Journal of School Leadership, 8,* 336–359.

Kramer, R. M., Brewer, M. B., & Hanna, B. A. (1996). Collective trust and collective action: The decision to trust as a social decision. In R. Kramer & T. Tyler (Eds.), *Trust in Organizations.* Thousand Oaks, CA: Sage.

Parsons, T. (1967). Some ingredients of a general theory of formal organization. In W. Halpin (Ed.), *Administrative theory in education* (pp. 40–72). New York: MacMillan.

Robinson, S. L. (1996). Trust and breach of the psychological contract. *Administrative Science Quarterly, 41*, 574–599.

Shaw, R. B. (1997). *Trust in the balance: Building successful organizations on results, integrity and concern.* San Francisco: Jossey-Bass.

Smith, P. A., Hoy, W. A., & Sweetland, S. R. (2001, March). Organizational health of high schools and dimensions of faculty trust. *Journal of School Leadership, 11*(2), 135–151.

Tarter, C. J., Sabo, D., & Hoy, W. K. (1995). Middle school climate, faculty trust, and effectiveness: A path analysis. *Journal of Research and Development in Education, 29*(1), 41–49.

14

Case Study #4: The Role of Principal Commitment in Creating Learning Communities

Gayle Moller

Schools across the United States are inundated with demands to change, or are they? Surely, the low-performing schools are bombarded by the media, the politicians, and the central office to change their schools to better meet the needs of their students as measured by test scores. The accountability push to move students who are failing to higher levels of achievement is evident in every state. Federal and state grants set these schools at a priority level for receiving resources.

However, while the majority of school staffs are anxious about the testing of their students, in reality there is little pressure to change for those schools that report satisfactory achievement on standardized tests. These schools have staff that are comfortable in the knowledge that, as long as their students achieve, most parents will be supportive of the type of teaching and learning that happens within the school. If the parents were dissatisfied, they would search the real estate pages in the local newspaper for homes located near schools that would match their expectations. Why should the school change? The teachers are succeeding with their students based on the accepted measurement, the school looks and acts like the school the parents attended, and there is no external pressure to change.

Unfortunately, the traditional schools of today may be succeeding with yesterday's model, but they are not preparing students for the world of tomorrow. The level of education the students need to acquire is not reflected in the curriculum of the past; it demands knowledge and skills that even most teachers do not have. The retooling of the teaching force is an enormous challenge that is ignored as schools continue to operate as if there were no need for change.

The most promising approach for helping teachers learn new knowledge and skills is the development of a professional learning community. Within schools that exhibit the dimensions of a professional learning community, the teachers are continuously improving their instructional practice based on data from their students. Teachers and other members of the school are actively engaged in ongoing, job-embedded professional development. Study groups, action research, and other forms of collaborative learning are the norm.

This case study examines the complexity of initiating a professional learning community within a school that does not have the external pressure to make substantive change. Teachers, parents, the community, and even the central office administration view this school as exemplary. The premise of initiating a professional learning community is to engage the professional staff in the study of the school to ensure that teaching results in improved student learning. How does a principal approach school reform if the professional staff is satisfied with the current status of the school?

The principal in this school is challenged with how to promote change when he perceives that everyone is comfortable with the existing system. In the current structure of schools, the principal is inordinately influential in the success or failure of any initiative. The day-to-day nuances of leadership are reflected in the overall culture of the school. The school in this case study has a traditional leadership structure, and the principal is the key player in promoting change.

KEY AREAS FOR REFLECTION

- Focus of teacher learning in the school
- Level of leadership commitment
- Relationship between principal and staff
- Types of support systems needed to ensure teacher development
- Influence of external change agent

THE CASE

Bedford Middle School is located in the mountains of a southeastern state. Although the school system is considered rural, it resides in a community that borders a medium-sized city, which is the only city of its size in this region of the state. Bedford Middle School is one of four middle schools within a county school system. With a student population of 730, the school's ethnic composition is 92% white, 4.8% Hispanic, 1.3% African American, and a small number of Native American and Asian American students. The school's Hispanic population is small but growing. This school is typical of the region's demographics, with the exception of the population in the nearby larger city. High-stakes accountability testing is taken seriously at this school, and the pressure of achieving expected outcomes results in a continual concern for teachers. In spite of the anxiety, this school has been repeatedly successful as measured by the state.

The socioeconomic level of the school is reflected in the 30% of students participating in the free-and-reduced lunch program. Most of the students live in middle-class homes with comfortable living conditions. Yet some of the students live outside the community surrounding the school where poverty is evident. Several of the teachers drive the school buses and have described the conditions in which these less advantaged students live. One teacher suggested that he would like to take the faculty on a bus ride to see where their students live so that they would understand why learning is often not a student's first priority.

The school building was constructed in 1972, is well maintained, and sits on a beautiful rolling hill that stretches to a two-lane street, which becomes a traffic nightmare at dismissal time as doting parents arrive to collect their children. The principal and staff work each afternoon to direct the traffic. These staff members are often opening the car doors to whisk students into their parents' waiting vehicles. During the process, they make contact with the parents through cordial greetings. The aggravation of the parents subsides as the staff extends this courtesy.

The faculty reflects a continuum of experience from 6 beginning teachers to 25 teachers who have more than 15 years teaching experience. The staff (100% white) reflect the majority students' ethnicity. In this right-to-work state, the teachers are reluctant to create problems because there is no teachers' union to advocate for their rights. Although staff may be reluctant to express their concerns, there continues to be a low turnover rate of staff in this school.

As one walks through the hallways at the beginning of the school day, there is the normal teeming of middle school students, but, as classes begin, there are relatively few students in the halls due to the 90-minute block schedule. Although many of the students recognize the value of the block schedule for their learning, they would prefer to be in the hallways more often making social contacts, a typical characteristic of children in the middle school years.

The principal, Sam Wilson, is presently in his second year of the principalship. He was selected to lead the school after serving five years in the role of assistant principal in this same school. Although it is unusual to promote an assistant principal to the principalship within the same school, the superintendent believed that Sam would be the best choice for the school. The faculty was familiar with Sam and, on the whole, they were satisfied with the selection.

As a learner, Sam found out about the professional learning community project through a colleague at the local university. He was enthusiastic about the school being selected to work with a facilitator to initiate this concept. Sam actively recruited Sharon Downey, an educator not on the school's staff, who would be the school's facilitator.

Although Sam had little information about the project, he knew that the teachers would need a block of time during the school day to work together as a professional learning community. Since he planned to schedule the school on a block schedule for the next school year, the logical solution was to build in common planning time for the teachers. Amid the hectic pace at the end of the school year, Sam shared the idea of the project and the use of planning time with the teachers. However, during the next year the faded memories of this conversation resulted in the majority of the teachers claiming that these changes were mandated and that they had little input.

Sharon's first contact with the whole faculty at the beginning of the school year was during their first meeting. Sam asked her to work with the staff in understanding the Myers-Briggs instrument, which he had recently completed in a university course and saw this as a way for Sharon to make entry with the staff. The meeting was well received by the staff, and it was revealed that Sam's type (Myers-Briggs) was not shared by anyone on the staff. This led to humorous comments that foreshadowed the evolution of Sam's relationship with the staff over the next two years.

As Sam and Sharon talked about the focus of a professional learning community, it was evident that, except for the focus on achieving satisfactory test scores, the teachers had not collaborated in the past about student learning. As a first step, they agreed that Sharon would visit with each team to find out what concerns the teachers and staff members had. Through focus groups, Sharon discovered a staff that deeply cared about the students they taught and were intuitively concerned about the students' lack of ability to think critically and their lack of interest in reading. The teachers also had faced a number of substantive changes this school year, and the stress was evident.

Sharon shared the major themes from the focus groups with Sam and they both decided that the next staff development day should be designed to address the issues. Two months later the entire staff held a retreat at a local facility. During this day, the teachers examined the themes from the focus groups and the changes that had taken place from the beginning of the school year. Sharon encouraged Sam to address the issues with the entire staff. This was a risk for both Sam and Sharon, but it appeared to be the best approach to "clear the air." Sam was asked to speak to concerns in a mock interview conducted by Sharon. The faculty was stunned that Sam was honest about his feelings, and they listened intently. Following this interview, the teachers rolled up their sleeves and worked together to figure out how they could work on the identified need: reading comprehension. The next day at school, Sam received compliments on his openness at the meeting.

During the next month teachers collected data from the students regarding their interests in reading. The data were summarized, and a small team agreed to learn how to facilitate study groups. Sam came to the training, but he was frequently called out of the group's meetings. The teachers worked through the strategy and agreed to present it to the faculty on their next staff development day.

Sharon did not attend the presentation of the model, but she heard about its success during her next visit from the principal and the team members. Of course, later she also heard from other teachers who felt they were being mandated to do something they did not understand. Sharon approached Sam and asked what his involvement was with the project. He said that he was supportive, but he was unable to give it much attention because there was a new superintendent in the school system and his "plate was full." He wished there were funding to release a teacher to help nurture the learning communities. When Sharon asked him what role he thought he should play, Sam said that he was reluctant to visit the learning communities because his presence would inhibit their work.

The acquiescent staff went through the motions of meeting, recording their discussions, and dutifully filing them in notebooks. It became painfully evident to Sharon that this perfunctory attention to the study group model was causing problems within the school. No one in the school was nurturing the teachers' involvement, and if a team succeeded, there was no recognition. Sam claimed that the school had no crisis to force the teachers to take the professional learning community seriously. What was he to do?

To address the growing concern of the groups, Sharon suggested to Sam that she again meet with the teams in a focus-group setting to collect data about the issues. In addition, Sharon applied for a small grant to cover the cost of a retreat for a representative from each team to work with Sharon and Sam to plan for next year.

The data from the focus groups were grouped again into thematic concerns. For two days Sam, Sharon, and the eight teachers struggled to find answers to the school's major concerns. Out of the meeting came a plan for starting the new school year with a response to the teachers' issues that was a compromise and yet continued the expectation that they would work together in learning communities. Sam was not pleased with the compromise, a reduction in the required meeting time, but he agreed to support the teachers' decisions. Everyone left with an understanding that this team would present their ideas at the first faculty meeting.

Summer is a time of respite, but it also allows memories to fade. At the end of the school year, the school council chairperson, a key player in the professional learning community project, decided to move out of the leadership role. The faculty voted for a new chairperson, who was one of the most vocal critics of the project. The principal and the former chairperson both met with the new leader over the summer to share their hopes for a more productive year.

The first faculty meeting came, and Sam made a decision to present the "message" from the new superintendent to the staff. Through a Power-Point presentation, Sam was honest about the demands of the superintendent, who felt that he had to take control of a school system that had "slackers." Following this lengthy presentation, Sam turned the meeting over to the new leader of the team whom he had met at the beginning of the summer. The message from this teacher leader was "drowned out" by the expectations of the superintendent.

Sharon asked Sam what happened, and he explained that he felt he needed to be honest with the staff about the new leadership in the school district. When Sharon asked the teachers about the message, most of them could not even remember what was said. She realized that the plans from the retreat were subsumed under Sam's desire to build a positive relationship with the superintendent.

Trying to approach the school from another angle, Sharon asked Sam about the data within the school that might help the teachers understand the learning needs of the students. Sam had provided some data for the team that attempted to implement study groups, and Sharon soon realized that the teachers had never seen the data before.

Realizing that the new leader of the School Council was interested in data, Sharon suggested to Sam that she work with this person to lay out a plan for collecting and analyzing data. Sam agreed and provided the teacher with one day to work with Sharon. The teacher leader was excited about the possibility of working with the data and, in fact, shared how she had analyzed data from her own students. It was evident that the teacher leader had the skills and interest to pursue this avenue. At the end of the day, Sam joined Sharon and the teacher leader to hear their plan. As Sam listened, Sharon noticed a lack of interest on his part and wondered what had happened to draw his attention away from the success of the project.

Weeks went by, and Sharon inquired about the next steps in the data collection. She checked with the teacher leader, who said Sam had never followed through on the ideas. When Sharon confronted Sam about his waning interest in working with the professional learning communities project, he shared stresses he was facing in his job. Some of the worries were internal, such as resistant teachers, and others were demands from the new superintendent.

THE CHALLENGE

If you were Sharon, what would you do to work with Sam and the school staff?

KEY QUESTIONS

1. Identify the key obstacles Sharon is facing in working with this school.
2. What keeps Sam from his commitment to this project?
3. How did the new superintendent set the stage for this principal's new perspective?
4. Could the teachers take on the leadership role to make the project a success?
5. What external pressures exist that might influence the school in the future to examine data to identify student learning needs?
6. Sam said that he believed in the project. What makes you suspicious of this statement?
7. Why is it difficult to influence teachers in this school to change?

SUGGESTED READINGS

Berliner, D. C., & Biddle, B. J. (1995). *The manufactured crisis: Myths, fraud, and the attack on America's public schools.* Reading, MA: Addison-Wesley.

Darling-Hammond, L. (1996). The quiet revolution: Rethinking teacher development. *Educational Leadership, 53*(6), 4–10.

Hawley, W. D., & Valli, L. (1999). The essentials of effective professional development: A new consensus. In L. Darling-Hammond and G. Sykes (Eds.), *Teaching as the learning profession* (pp. 127–150). San Francisco: Jossey-Bass.

Hoerr, T. R. (1996). Collegiality: A new way to define instructional leadership. *Phi Delta Kappan, 77*(5), 380–381.

Lambert, L. (1998). *Building leadership capacity in schools.* Alexandria, VA: Association for Supervision and Curriculum Development.

Louis, K. S., Kruse, S. D., & Marks, H. M. (1996). Schoolwide professional community. In Fred Newmann and Associates (Eds.), *Authentic achievement: Restructuring schools for intellectual quality* (pp. 179–204). San Francisco: Jossey-Bass.

Morrissey, M. S. (2000). *Professional learning communities: An ongoing exploration.* Austin, TX: Southwest Educational Development Laboratory.

Wood, F. H., & Killian, J. (1998). Job-embedded learning makes the difference in school improvement. *Journal of Staff Development, 19*(1), 52–54.

15

Case Study #5: Reculturing a School in Crisis

Dianne F. Olivier

The call for school reform is not new to educators. Over the past 20 years, major reform movements in the educational field have followed a cyclical pattern of responding to external pressure for change in the educational system (Cuban, 1990). The 1960s emphasized innovations to improve schooling outcomes; the 1970s called for increased public accountability for dollars spent on education; and the 1980s demanded educational excellence through a multitude of federal and state commission reports (Weller & Weller, 1997). In the late 1980s, *restructuring* became a key word in educational reform to characterize change deemed necessary in the organizational structure of schools to achieve the nation's goals for educational quality (Peterson, McCarthy, & Elmore, 1996). The challenge of the 1990s and the entrance into the twenty-first century has been to alter the fundamental ways in which organizations are designed, thus affecting the culture and structure of schools (Fullan, 1991), as well as redesigning teaching and learning and goals for schooling (Darling-Hammond, 1993). This shift supports the development of a new practice of *whole-school* change that is consistent with an understanding of how organizations change and how learning takes place (Wagner, 1998).

Sirotnik (1989) maintained that schools should not be viewed as targets of educational reform and improvement. Rather, they should be recognized as centers for educational change, serving as centers of inquiry where educators in schools become their own change agents. In these settings they "become active and critical consumers of their own and others' knowledge in the context of their own practices and the changing of these practices" (p. 107), thereby creating an organization from within.

The continual search for more effective strategies for school improvement has led to new models. Some of these rely heavily upon findings in the fields of human relations and organizational theory, such as the concept of a professional learning community (PLC). As in the development of a PLC, the literature from these two fields asserts that reform efforts take time to implement and must be sustained in the organization (Weller & Weller, 1997) to affect school change and student learning. Sergiovanni (1994) proposed that a school be viewed as a community with shared ideas, in which bonding between people takes place and behavior is exercised through norms, purposes, values, professional socialization, collegiality, and natural interdependence. Implicit within this notion of community is the factor of school culture, and particularly the interpersonal interactions and social processes that shape that culture (Cavanagh & Dellar, 1997). Changing school cultures can be very challenging because it entails altering long-held beliefs, expectations, and habits, and developing collective values and norms. Hargreaves (1995) noted that developing collaborative cultures entails *reculturing* the school from a focus on individual teachers or balkanized teacher subgroups.

This case examines the challenges of reculturing undertaken by one principal at a school deemed in crisis. Many teachers are comfortable with the status quo and reluctant to move toward change, while others acknowledge signs of a troubled school. After struggling and achieving only minimal success, the principal's intent is to reculture the school applying the dimensions of a professional learning community.

KEY AREAS OF REFLECTION

- Shaping a school's culture (reculturing)
- Collegial relationships
- External support systems
- Professional commitment
- Barriers to change

THE CASE

Live Oaks Elementary is located in a rural community in a southeastern state, which is beginning to see a decrease in its overall population. While the community attracts tourists to its historical sites, new businesses are minimal. The long-time major employer, a clothing operation, recently relocated its business out of the country, significantly increasing the unemployment rate within the community.

Live Oaks Elementary, composed of grades 4–6, maintains a population of approximately 600 students, of which 66% are African American, 33% are white, and 1% are Asian American and Hispanic. Live Oaks has a high percentage of economically disadvantaged students at 82.3%. The staff comprises 32 professional teachers, a curriculum coordinator, a behavior interventionist, and a reading facilitator. The community recognizes Live Oaks as one of the district's *low-performing* schools.

When Debbie Bergeron, the current principal, arrived at Live Oaks Elementary in 1997, she entered a school facing multiple crises, including high staff turnover and low student achievement. She quickly came to recognize that these crises resulted from a school culture that reinforced teachers' beliefs that they were not ultimately responsible for student learning. Live Oaks Elementary faced high rates of teacher and administrative turnover, high absentee rates for teachers and students, severe disciplinary problems, teacher isolation, low expectations, and high failure rates. Additionally, the community maintained little trust in the school's ability to meet the needs of the students. In the 10 years before Debbie arrived, six predecessors had entered and left the principal's post experiencing little success in improving the school.

The year Debbie became principal, several teachers had retired, resigned, or transferred out of the school (some voluntarily, others not). Although her predecessor had filled a few positions, Debbie was presented with the task of interviewing and recommending the appointment of eight new staff members immediately prior to the opening of the school year. Live Oaks was Debbie's first administrative position; thus, the experience of selecting teachers was a challenge. Her intent was to select knowledgeable, energetic teachers who would infuse new blood into a stagnant faculty.

After addressing these staffing concerns, Debbie looked to student performance and developed a plan to remedy the many academic shortcomings.

In this effort, she had to contend with incomplete records regarding achievement data, the school budget, and school and district policies and procedures. She inherited the disarray from the previous principal, who had been released of his duties due to poor performance for instructional leadership and overall administrative duties. As Debbie began to observe classes and review lesson plans, she immediately noted alarming inconsistency in teacher planning, preparation, and presentation of the required academic curriculum.

Prior to becoming a principal at Live Oaks, Debbie had been recognized as an outstanding elementary teacher and as a specialist in the state teacher assessment program. Thus, she relied on the strengths she had developed as a teacher and spent countless hours in classroom observation assessing instruction using the components of effective teaching. Debbie had hoped that her in-depth observations would serve as a positive influence in promoting teaching and learning, but instead, she faced extreme resistance from the majority of teachers. Many teachers expected and accepted low student achievement, yet failed to assume responsibility to improve instruction, an attitude carried over from past principals who were not visible in classrooms and consistently awarded teachers with ratings of satisfactory despite their performance.

In contrast, Debbie's classroom observations reflected specific lesson areas and teaching methods deemed in need of improvement. She documented those areas and rated some teachers' performance as unsatisfactory. As a result, many teachers expressed dissatisfaction that their methods and strategies were questioned and were outraged at documentation of unsatisfactory performance on evaluations.

While Debbie's teacher evaluations were unpopular, they clearly communicated the need for improvement and change. Through day-to-day interactions with faculty and observations of the dynamics among faculty members, Debbie noted a lack of trust among teachers and with the administration. This level of distrust prevented the school from progressing. Discussions of ongoing school procedures or ideas presented by the principal resulted in virtually little or no dialogue among the staff. Teachers openly displayed negative attitudes and skepticism.

Live Oaks Elementary operated with a minimal administrative staff with teacher leaders assuming the roles of curriculum coordinator and reading facilitator. After carefully assessing the operations within the school, Debbie and the support staff realized there was a need to create opportunities to foster collaboration and teaming, thus reducing teacher isolation. Although initial attempts were dire, the opportunities provided by grade and content levels slowly began to impact the professional staff. The teachers gradually began to accept the notion that together they could alter the status of Live Oaks Elementary.

Debbie and her immediate support staff were open to suggestions and received continued support and assistance from the superintendent and central office staff. When she discovered that the school leadership team existed on paper only, she restructured it to reflect representation from all grade levels and programs within the school. The new leadership team became involved in sessions that stressed administrative and teacher leadership, school improvement planning, and a focus on student performance — especially the performance of those students deemed most at risk of failure.

While several teachers began to accept the challenge to improve the academic status of the school, a small group of teachers thwarted any and all attempts at progress. These saboteurs formed a vocal minority that managed to diffuse forward progress. They believed the low performance of students was preordained by student socioeconomic status and lack of parental involvement. They resented a principal who promoted change and who maintained that the teaching processes being used played a critical role in the academic success or failure of students. These teachers felt that the obstacles they faced were far greater than their ability to impact students positively.

Concurrently, a tragedy occurred within the Live Oaks family. One of the new young teachers was killed in an automobile accident while returning home from school. The staff was profoundly affected by the loss of this energetic and enthusiastic teacher. The tension among teachers and with the administration softened in the aftermath of this tragic incident.

While the entire first year seemed to present a struggle for Debbie, she was enthusiastic to begin year two. Test scores were still significantly below state and district averages. However, the extensive training recently initiated in the area of reading raised hopes for improving low reading levels of students. Prior to the beginning of Debbie's second year, it became quite clear that she would again begin the school year with a large percentage of new teachers. Some resisters elected to move to other positions outside of Live Oaks or retire; thus, 15 new faculty members were hired. Debbie hoped these new teachers were willing to assume the current challenges.

The implementation of a scientifically, research-based reading program allowed teachers to strategize and plan for students at their specific reading levels. A new school norm, the 90-minute reading block, became sacred. There were no interruptions from outside or within the school, and all teachers and students were actively involved in a structured reading program. Results surfaced immediately. Although the faculty was aware that significant improvement schoolwide would take time, pockets of progress became evident. Attendance rates among teachers began to improve, and a new emphasis was placed on student attendance. Failure rates of students began to decline, and a slight decrease in disciplinary referrals emerged.

In the midst of ongoing changes, Live Oaks Elementary became involved in a project through the Southwest Educational Development Laboratory aimed at developing a PLC. This project was designed to develop teacher leaders and assist Debbie and her support staff through the provision of schoolwide improvement strategies. The significant opportunity was offered to the principal and the school. Live Oaks Elementary accepted and became involved in a project aimed at developing a professional learning community. This opportunity through the Southwest Educational Development Laboratory would foster shared leadership skills through developing teacher leaders, and would assist Debbie and her support staff through the provision of strategies to address schoolwide improvement.

In the fall, the faculty completed a Professional Learning Community questionnaire, which assessed the perceptions of the school staff as a learning organization in terms of shared leadership, shared vision and values, collective learning and application, supportive conditions, and shared personal practice. The results indicated that the school rated itself high on the component of collective learning. In reality, a minimal amount of collective learning occurred as a voluntary action among staff members, but was imposed through district and state mandates. Teachers had yet to reach the desired level of trust that would support collective assessment of their work and dialogue around learning.

Debbie's second year ended with some indication of continued positive movement, yet some issues were unresolved. The new reading program increased collegial work through reading component meetings, lesson preparation sessions, inter-classroom visits, and modeling among teachers. However, distrust still existed among certain faculty members. Continued resistance to change was evidenced by a tendency to resort to old teaching methods behind closed doors.

At the close of the year, the school received its accountability rating from the state and was disappointed to acknowledge their status as Academically Below Average. Although teachers were disappointed at the school's label after a year of hard work and visible improvement, they believed that they could make progress in meeting the academic needs of the students. The teachers made a commitment to incorporate new strategies promoted through the PLC project even though their progress was deemed minimal. Most staff trusted that they were moving in the right direction. Teachers now believed that, regardless of the obstacles they faced, they could indeed impact student performance.

The new school year for Live Oaks Elementary began in a very smooth and orderly manner, with an increasingly experienced and trusted principal. However, another large turnover of teachers created the need to prepare new staff to implement the strategies and methods recently adopted at Live Oaks. Professional development sessions were designed to address the needs of the new teachers and to revitalize those experienced teachers.

A staff development session titled True Colors sparked interest and served as a breakthrough in the area of collaboration and collective learning. This session, conducted by two faculty members, provided an opportunity for teachers to explore their own learning styles and to formulate plans that would foster collaboration. This session served as a critical incident for the staff upon which additional success could emerge.

Lingering issues of concern were also addressed. *Crisis Prevention Intervention* helped teachers tackle severe disciplinary disruptions through nonviolent methods of intervention in potentially explosive situations. *In Touch with Parents* strengthened the level and depth of active parent participation through developing teacher-parent collaboration to enhance student learning. Training and refresher sessions for new teachers and experienced teachers in reading and math standards enhanced the school's focus on student improvement.

As a recipient of a state grant for low-performing schools, Live Oaks Elementary was invited to participate in a State School Improvement Conference. A core group representing the school, district, school board, and community participated. The conference featured national speakers and small group sessions allowing school teams to plan collaboratively for the new school session. Live Oaks team members returned and enthusiastically shared information with the entire faculty. Several strategies emerged to assist students, primarily in the areas of tutorial programs, discipline, parent contacts, and effective implementation of the reading program.

At a schoolwide staff development session, two teachers reviewed the school's progress toward becoming a PLC. While the model of the PLC had not been overtly highlighted as the model for school improvement, the principal and support staff had been incorporating activities and methods in support of this model. The presentation was extremely well received, as the majority of staff voiced a commitment to change. Their renewed interest and excitement in working toward success seemed to permeate the faculty. There were more teamwork and collaboration in planning and assessing than had previously been observed.

To address the continuing low performance scores on state tests, the staff elected to participate in a comprehensive school review process designed to assess perceptions regarding satisfaction with overall school performance. The questionnaires, interviews, and focus groups produced pertinent information deemed valuable in planning for school improvement. Teachers reported being dissatisfied with being labeled as a low-performing school and revealed displeasure with those teachers who attempted to diffuse strategies toward change. They were also disturbed with the negative perceptions within the community and committed to changing them. Findings also revealed a need for leadership stability at the administrative and teacher levels, which faculty believed adversely affected student performance.

Parents reported high expectations for their children and expressed that the school was not adequately meeting their children's needs. Conversely, teachers' perceptions reflected lower expectations for students and assurance that they were achieving all that was possible given the seemingly insurmountable needs of the students. The students candidly expressed displeasure with less-important policies, such as school uniforms, to more in-depth concerns relating to ineffective teaching methods and responsibility for student learning.

After a tremendous amount of work, spring testing was right around the corner, and teachers and students were apprehensive. Although content standards were being addressed, more time was needed for preparing the students for the test. The teachers at Live Oaks had rallied to the challenge. Their school had instituted the most comprehensive tutoring program throughout the district, with 16 teachers involved in the after-school tutorial program. But was this enough?

Prior to receiving the results regarding student performance, the faculty at Live Oaks took an unexpected turn. After the faculty had been implementing the schoolwide reading program, they were requested to vote on the continuation of the program. Much to the surprise of the principal, the 80% approval rating by the faculty was not sustained. While 60% of the teachers wanted to continue the reading program, 40% expressed dissatisfaction and wanted to eliminate it and revert to their old ways.

Debbie and the teacher support team were disheartened by the vote. Why would teachers discard a program in which students were succeeding? The superintendent met with a Leadership Team reflecting representatives throughout the school to discuss reasons for discontent with the research-based reading program. While few teachers openly expressed their feelings, some mentioned the stringent requirements and extensive amounts of teacher preparation necessary to implement the program according to guidelines. The superintendent requested that the Leadership Team think seriously about the consequences of abandoning the program. He also challenged the team to discuss alternatives that would replace the reading program if needed.

The end-of-the-year test results indicated movement toward improvement! Seventy percent of the fourth-grade students passed the language arts test, an increase of 5%, and 64% of the students were successful on the mathematics test, a dramatic 30-point increase over the 34% success rate previously. The marked increase in student performance, combined with improved student attendance, contributed to a significant increase in the school's performance scores, which surpassed other district elementary schools.

THE CHALLENGE

If you were Debbie, how would you continue to ensure that the school's focus remains on student achievement and doesn't revert to the "old ways"?

KEY QUESTIONS

1. Assess Debbie's methods for addressing division among staff members.

2. Identify critical incidents that fostered collaborative relationships among faculty members.
3. Identify the continuing barriers that challenge Debbie.
4. Offer recommendations for tackling the issue of faculty instability.
5. How does the administration and faculty continue to deal with the issue of trust?
6. In order for Live Oaks to move toward a culture of PLC, how would the beliefs and values need to change to develop a sense of shared responsibility for student learning?
7. Identify initial steps in the reculturing process. Discuss next steps considering the role of the principal, teachers, students, parents, and the community.

SUGGESTED READINGS

Cavanagh, R. F., & Dellar, G. B. (1997). *School culture: A quantitative perspective on a subjective phenomenon.* Paper presented at the annual meeting of the American Educational Research Association, Chicago.

Cuban, L. (1988). Why do some reforms persist? *Educational Administration Quarterly, 23,* 329–335.

Cuban, L. (1990). Reforming again, again, and again. *Educational Researcher, 19*(1), 3–13.

Darling-Hammond, L. (1993, June). Reframing the school reform agenda: Developing capacity for school transformation. *Phi Delta Kappan, 74*(10), 752–761.

Fullan, M. (1991). *The new meaning of educational change.* New York: Teachers College Press.

Hargreaves, A. (1995, April). Renewal in the age of paradox. *Educational Leadership, 52*(7), 14–19.

Hoy, W. K., & Miskel, C. G. (1996). *Educational administration: Theory, research and practice* (5th ed.). New York: McGraw-Hill.

Joyce, B., & Calhoun, E. (1995, April). School renewal: An inquiry, not a formula. *Educational Leadership, 52*(7), 51–55.

Peterson, P. L., McCarthy, S. J., & Elmore, R. F. (1996, Spring). Learning from school restructuring. *American Educational Research Journal, 33*(1), 119–153.

Sergiovanni, T. J. (1994). *Building community in schools.* San Francisco: Jossey-Bass.

Sirotnik, K. A. (1989). The school as the center of change. In T. J. Sergiovanni & H. H. Moore (Eds.), *Schooling for tomorrow: Directing reforms to issues that count.* Boston: Allyn & Bacon.

Wagner, T. (1998, March). Change as collaborative inquiry: A constructivist methodology for reinventing schools. *Phi Delta Kappan,* 512–517.

Weller, L. D., & Weller, S. J. (1997, October). Quality learning organizations and continuous improvement: Implementing the concept. *NAAPS Bulletin, 81*(591), 62–70.

5

FROM IMPLEMENTATION TO INSTITUTIONALIZATION

16

Lessons Learned

We are not where we want to be,
We are not where we are going to be,
But we are not where we were.

—Rosa Parks

One purpose of this book was to document and examine evidence of intentional efforts in schools that were actively engaged in creating PLCs using Hord's (1997a) approach. The authors selected exemplars and non-exemplars from 64 interviews across six diverse K–12 school settings that validated practices promoting and hindering school improvement efforts. Information was provided showing the progressive development evident in the schools moving from initiation to implementation in the change process. The six identified schools had moved through initiation and were working at various levels of implementation, with two schools reaching institutionalization.

The evidence supports the distinct yet overlapping nature and interdependency of each of the five PLC dimensions: shared and supportive leadership, shared values and visions, collective learning and application, shared personal practice, and supportive conditions. Moreover, the 22 critical attributes that emerged through data analysis reveal additional information and patterns that reconfigure and expand the Hord approach.

WHAT WE'VE LEARNED

Data from the current study reinforce the usefulness of the five dimensions and related attributes that appear in the Professional Learning Community Organizer (see figure 2.4) and in figure 16.1.

Similar to our prior research findings, the authors again found that the leadership of the principal was key (Hipp & Huffman, 2000). It is clear

- **Shared and Supportive Leadership**
  - o Nurturing leadership among staff
  - o Shared power, authority, and responsibility
  - o Broad-based decision making that reflects commitment and accountability

- **Shared Values and Vision**
  - o Espoused values and norms
  - o Focus on student learning
  - o High expectations
  - o Shared vision guides teaching and learning

- **Collective Learning and Application**
  - o Sharing information
  - o Seeking new knowledge, skills, and strategies
  - o Working collaboratively to plan, solve problems, and improve learning opportunities

- **Shared Personal Practice**
  - o Peer observations to offer knowledge, skills, and encouragement
  - o Feedback to improve instructional practices
  - o Sharing outcomes of instructional practices
  - o Coaching and mentoring

- **Supportive Conditions**
  - o Relationships
    - Caring relationships
    - Trust and respect
    - Recognition and celebration
    - Risk-taking
    - Unified effort to embed change
  - o Structures
    - Resources (time, money, materials, people)
    - Facilities
    - Communication systems

Figure 16.1. PLC dimensions and critical attributes.

that in schools where principals disperse power, invite input into decisions, and nurture the capabilities of all staff to focus on a common vision, school goals are more likely to be achieved. Sergiovanni (1992) described principals as leaders of leaders: "They work hard to build up the capacities and others, so that direct leadership will no longer be needed. This is achieved through team building, leadership development, shared decision making, and striving to establish the value of collegiality" (p. 123). Leaders must also be learners, as "leaders can influence restructuring by modeling the desired learning behaviors and by valuing the search for new ideas" (Walker & Sackney, 1999, p. 6). Walker and Sackney further this statement citing Sergiovanni's (1996) argument for leadership as pedagogy: "When leadership as pedagogy is practiced, principals exercise their stewardship responsibilities by committing themselves to building, serving, caring for, and protecting the school and its purposes" (p. xvi).

Unfortunately, we discovered that creating and sustaining a shared vision is not modeled effectively in any of the six schools, perhaps because a shared set of values is not apparent. Ideally, shared values would inspire a shared vision among diverse stakeholders, and student-focused decisions would be connected to site goals. This was not yet apparent in the six research schools. Insight is gained from Olivier, Cowan, and Pankake (2000) who found that although schools pay attention to many things, matters that make a difference, such as how schools operate to enhance student learning, are at times neglected. The development of shared values can serve to help staff identify what is vitally important. "A school can fulfill no higher purpose than to teach all its members that they can make what they believe in happen and to encourage them to contribute to and benefit from the leadership of others" (Barth, 1990a, p. 12).

In addition, the data indicates that it is difficult to separate the dimensions of collective learning and application and shared personal practice. Collective learning provides the opportunity for staff to collaborate and apply new knowledge, skills, and strategies. Teachers begin this process by engaging in sharing information and open dialogue. Shared personal practice involves more than simply observing and providing feedback; it often involves sharing outcomes of new practices in both formal and informal settings. Additionally, teachers make plans and solve problems based on student data. In essence, there exists interplay between these two dimensions that is cyclical in nature. Teachers learn together, apply what they have learned, reflect on the process, and in turn, discuss the results of their practices. At the institutionalization phase in shared personal practice, teachers analyze student work and revise instructional strategies. Thus, collective learning opens the door to continuous learning through shared personal practice.

Most importantly, we found supportive conditions to be the glue that is critical to hold the other dimensions together. Walker and Sackney (1999) viewed mature learning communities at the institutionalization level as "dynamic locations of extraordinary, but natural human excellence" where "elements of social cohesion, including trust, hope, and reciprocity, are ever present" (p. 24). Without creating a culture of trust, respect, and inclusiveness with a focus on relationships, even the most innovative means of finding time and resources and developing communication systems will have little effect on creating a community of learners. Davis (2002) supports this idea when he explains that community can only be sustained when individuals are *in relation* (italics added). He continues his explanation by describing the mutuality of relationships as being "personal, interactive and immediate" (p. 2). These interactions are active, not passive, and each person nurtures and cares about the other.

Finally, there were few references to student, parent, community, and central office involvement that incorporated adults and students deep within the organization, except in the schools at the highest level of implementation. Nonetheless, it is apparent that the entire school community — students, parents, community members, and central office staff — must be actively involved in collaborative efforts to achieve school goals and sustain efforts. "Community building calls us to take a curious approach to the world, a caring approach to students, teachers, and parents, and a problem solving approach to the challenges to contemporary schools" (Walker & Sackney, 1999, p. 27). We maintain that future school leaders need to create communities of learners that include broad-based leadership built on shared visions that emerge from the relationships, values, beliefs, and commitments of the entire organization. Further research needs to illuminate how to develop and sustain the interactions — not just give lip service or make half-hearted attempts to engage stakeholders in important school efforts.

RECENT RESEARCH

Two recent dissertations have augmented our study (Kopack Hill, 2002; Schmitt, 2002). Kopack Hill's (2002) research addressed the issue of designing an educational program for intermediate age students by creating a PLC that would ultimately become a *sustainable* learning organization. After one and a half years of planning to open a school and implementing the first year, the researcher principal found the essence of Hord's model was imbedded in six key attributes that were needed to create such a school community. These included: shared vision, shared leadership, team learning, attention to diversity, willingness to examine mental models, and systems/complex adaptive thinking. According to Kopack Hill, "It is imperative that educators become familiar with the concepts that form the foundation of these attributes" (p. 238). She subsequently argued that, in practice, the last three attributes are often neglected in school communities, thus contributing to the demise of the PLC.

As a result of her efforts, Kopack Hill challenged educators to find ways to "actively seek out diversity [all forms] both inside and outside the school buildings and engage in activities that help us learn from others who present divergent views" (p. 239). Further, she urged that educators must learn to become comfortable with the nonlinear and counterintuitive thinking that "takes us over the edge of understanding to an exploration of the unknown" (p. 240), thereby defying our traditional thinking. This author stressed that, for most, it is difficult to imagine expending the energy needed to build a PLC, while still maintaining a focus on creating one that will *sustain learning* long after the individuals of the school move on. It was concluded that these two efforts, *creating* and *sustaining* a PLC, need to take place simultaneously. Further, not doing so seems to ensure that the PLC will live only as long as the individuals who are participating are present.

Next, in a large Midwest high school that had worked purposefully to become a PLC and endured the test of sustainability, Schmitt (2002) found significant evidence of Hord's five dimensions in classrooms, meetings, and throughout school documents. He also identified an additional three factors that contributed to institutionalization: community connections, teacher-student relationships, and professional commitment. He cited broad-based evidence that strong community connections were apparent in numerous task forces, collective commitments from community members and parents who actively supported the school's vision, and relationships with colleges to assist students in transitioning after high school graduation. The strong network of relationships with feeder schools, area businesses, and colleges and universities reflected deep-seated bonds that supported the vision and mission of the school.

Schmitt also identified the importance of the teacher-student relationship as an essential element in successful student learning. One school director was heard telling a teacher that teaching was an equal balance between relationship and instruction. The final area, which sustained this "vibrant" professional learning community, was the professional commitment of teachers, administrators, and school board members over time. Schmitt's research revealed a passionate dedication to student learning by the entire school community and emphasized that a school's unique culture and setting determine the journey it will take.

SUMMARY

This book speaks to the heart of educational reform for the twenty-first century, and reveals findings for *a new approach* for school improvement that involves the entire professional staff in continuous learning and collaboration. Our research provides detailed information about the professional learning community dimensions and how school staffs operate as PLCs. Schools involved in sincere efforts to broaden the base of leadership to include teachers and administrators, to define shared vision based on student learning, and to provide a culture of continual support, will make great strides in becoming learning organizations and addressing critical student needs. Moreover, in an interview with Walker and Sackney (1999), Vivian Hajnal concluded that the nature and quality of leadership behavior, the existence of a collaborative culture, and the level of trust and staff involvement were critical factors in institutionalization and school effectiveness.

Building professional learning communities is a journey as reflected by the time and energy exerted to move schools from one phase to the next. Some schools move along in their efforts at a steady pace, while others seem to stall and proceed without reculturing (Fullan, 2000). Although school improvement plans need to be contextual and unique to the student population, there are strategies and efforts that can guide in fostering cultures that systematically address school improvement and student learning. We hope educators will use the new Professional Learning Community Assessment (PLCA) (see figure 8.1) to diagnose and evaluate PLC efforts.

To move to institutionalization, change cannot be individual and fragmented, but must be collaborative and embedded within the day-to-day work to address the needs of students (Louis & Marks, 1996). To meet the diverse needs of students requires people to change their attitudes and habits of action; thus change involves learning. People need to develop a capacity to continuously learn and to adapt to a variety of complex environments. Davis (2002) maintains the notion that community development is not an achievement or event; it is an *undertaking*. This undertaking requires resources, leadership, and continuous support to succeed and be meaningful throughout the entire school community.

As evidenced by our case studies, whether or not a school principal engages with the faculty and staff during an innovation or change effort can determine its success or failure. We anticipate our research will continue to uncover critical information relevant to managing change in schools. This research will deepen that understanding of change and assist leaders in guiding their schools to develop healthy cultures focused on student performance. Dufour and Eaker (1998) suggest, "Until educators can describe the school they are trying to create, it is impossible to develop policies, procedures, or programs that will help make that ideal a reality" (p. 64). We urge students and school leaders to consider using the Professional Learning Community Organizer (PLCO) (figure 2.4) to initiate, implement, and institutionalize school improvement efforts.

The information provided in this book, including the five case studies that have been presented, will prove useful in stimulating dialogue about developing PLCs in leadership preparation programs and among school staff. Our goals have been to present relevant research and the details of schools that are in the midst of substantive change. We provided a glimpse of each school's successes and challenges, and raised issues for you to consider. Each school's journey differs as to the uniqueness of the context, issues, and people, as will yours. How will you begin your journey?

Beyond dispute, the preparation of school administrators is key. Educational administration programs and other institutions of higher education need to prepare potential school leaders to move beyond issues of management, and provide practical experiences that focus on relationships and learning outcomes. These programs must teach future administrators how to facilitate school change centered on student and teacher learning. Leadership preparation programs must guide potential leaders in the following: developing a shared vision, establishing collaborative decision making, aligning the energies of diverse groups of people, supporting the interdependency of individuals in the organization, and providing opportunities for shared learning among staff.

Transformational principals can make a difference in student learning by influencing internal school processes, providing support, engaging teachers to fully participate in decision making, and developing a shared sense of responsibility. These efforts will equip staff members to improve the conditions for learning in schools (Davis, 1998). The principal's most significant effect on student learning comes through his or her efforts to establish a vision of the school and develop goals related to the accomplishment of the vision. Sharing leadership and aligning people to a vision is crucial and leads to a "leadership-centered culture . . . the ultimate act of leadership" (Kotter, 1990, p. 11).

"Organizations learn only through individuals who learn" (Senge, 1990, p. 139). Therefore, school leaders must establish conditions that encourage new ways of thinking and interacting to build capacity and schoolwide commitment to a shared vision. Learning evolves and must engage and nurture interdependent thinking in an environment where all people are connected and valued. "The organizations that will truly excel in the future will be the organizations that discover how to tap people's commitment and capacity to learn at all levels in an organization" (Senge, 1990, p. 4). Finally, school administrators need to expand their paradigms of leadership. As Lambert (1998) stated in her book, *Building Leadership Capacity in Schools*,

> School leadership needs to be a broad concept that is separated from person, role, and a discreet set of individual behaviors. It needs to be embedded in the school community as a whole. Such a broadening of the concept of leadership suggests shared responsibility for a shared purpose of community. (p. 5)

Or as Rost (1993) proposed, "Leadership is an influence relationship among leaders and followers who intend real changes that reflects their mutual purposes" (p. 102). The challenge for school leaders in this millennium is to guide their school communities from concept to capability—a capability that is self-sustaining and that will institutionalize reform—*A New Approach*.

References

Argyris, C. (1990). *Overcoming organizational defenses: Facilitating organizational learning*. Upper Saddle River, NJ: Prentice Hall.

Argyris, C. (1993). *Knowledge for action: A guide to overcoming barriers to organizational change*. San Francisco: Jossey-Bass.

Ashton, P. (1984). Teacher efficacy: A motivational paradigm for effective teacher education. *Journal of Teacher Education, 35*(5), 28–32.

Astuto, T. A., Clark, D. L., Read, A. M., McGree, K., & Fernandez, L. K. (1993). *Challenges to dominant assumptions controlling educational reform*. Andover, MA: Regional Laboratory for the Educational Improvement of the Northeast and Island.

Barth, R. S. (1990a). *Improving schools from within*. San Francisco: Jossey-Bass.

Barth, R. S. (1990b). A personal vision of a good school. *Phi Delta Kappan, 71*(7), 512–516.

Begley, P. T., & Johansson, O. (2000). *Using what we know about values: Promoting authentic leadership and democracy in schools*. Paper presented at the annual UCEA Conference, Albuquerque, NM.

Block, P. (1993). *Stewardship: Choosing services over self-interest*. San Francisco: Berrett-Koehler.

Boyd, V. (1992). *School context: Bridge or barrier to change?* Austin, TX: Southwest Educational Development Laboratory.

Brandt, R. (1995). On restructuring schools: A conversation with Fred Newmann. *Educational Leadership, 53*(3), 70–73.

Brown, D. (1990). *Decentralization and school-based management*. Bristol, PA: Falmer Press.

Brown, D. F. (1995). Experiencing shared leadership: Teacher's reflections. *Journal of School Leadership, 5*(4), 334–355.

Bryk, A. S., Easton, J. Q., Kerbow, D., Rollow, S. G., & Sebring, P. A. (1994). The state of Chicago school reform. *Phi Delta Kappan, 76*(1), 74–78.

Calderon, M. (1998). *TLCs—Teachers' learning communities: Training manual.* Baltimore: CRESPAR, Johns Hopkins University.

Cavanagh, R. F., & Dellar, G. B. (1997*). School culture: A quantitative perspective on a subjective phenomenon.* Paper presented at the annual meeting of the American Educational Research Association, Chicago.

Charters, W. W., Jr., & Jones, J. E. (1973, November). On the risk of appraising nonevents in program evaluation. *Educational Researcher, 2*(11), 5–7.

Chin, R., & Benne, K. D. (1969). General strategies for effecting changes in human systems. In W. G. Bennis, K. D. Benne, & R. Chin (Eds.), *The planning of change* (2nd ed.) (pp. 32–59). London: Holt, Rinehart & Winston.

Comer, J. (1988*). Quantitative methods for public administration: Techniques and application.* Fort Worth, TX: Harcourt Brace.

Cowan, D., & Hord, S. M. (1999). *Reflections on school renewal and communities of continuous inquiry and improvement.* Paper presented at the annual meeting of the American Educational Research Association, Montreal, Canada.

Cuban, L. (1990). Reforming again, again, and again. *Educational Researcher, 19*(1), 3–13.

Darling-Hammond, L. (1990). Teacher professionalism: Why and how. In A. Lieberman (Ed.), *Schools as collaborative cultures* (pp. 25–50). Bristol, PA: Falmer Press.

Darling-Hammond, L. (1993, June). Reframing the school reform agenda: Developing capacity for school transformation. *Phi Delta Kappan, 74*(10), 752–761.

Darling-Hammond, L. (1996). The quiet revolution: Rethinking teacher development. *Educational Leadership, 53*(6), 4–10.

Davidson, B. M., & Dell, G. L. (1996). *Transforming teachers' work: The impact of two principals' leadership styles.* Paper presented at the annual meeting of the American Educational Research Association, New York.

Davis, O. L., Jr. (2002). Editorial on community. *Journal of Curriculum and Supervision, 18*(1),1–3.

Davis, S. H. (1998). Taking aim at effective leadership. *Thrust for Educational Leadership, 28*(2), 6–9.

Deal, T. E., & Kennedy, A. A. (1982). *Corporate cultures.* Reading, MA: Addison-Wesley.

Deming, W. E. (1986). *Out of crisis.* Cambridge, MA: MIT Center for Advanced Engineering Study.

Dewey, J. (1938). *Experience and education.* New York: Macmillan Company, Collier Books, in cooperation with Kappa Delta Pi.

DuFour, R., & Eaker, R. (1998). *Professional learning communities at work: Best practices for enhancing student achievement.* Bloomington, IN: National Educational Service.

Dunne, F., & Honts, F. (1998). *That group really makes me think! Critical friends groups and the development of reflective practitioners.* Paper presented at the annual meeting of the American Educational Research Association, San Diego.

Eaker, R., DuFour, R., & Burnette, R. (2002). *Getting started: Reculturing schools to become professional learning communities.* Bloomington, IN: National Educational Service.

Edmonds, R. R. (1979, October). Effective schools for the urban poor. *Educational Leadership, 37*(2), 15–24.

Elmore, R. F. (Winter 1999/2000). Building a new structure for school leadership. *American Educator, 23*(4), 6–13.

Firestone, W. A. (1996). Images of teaching and proposals for reform: A comparison of ideas from cognitive and organizational research. *Educational Administration Quarterly, 32*(2), 209–235.

Foster, R., & Suddards, C. (1999). *Leadership within high school communities: A multiple study perspective.* Paper presented at the annual meeting of the American Educational Research Association, Montreal, Canada.

Fullan, M. (1985). Change processes and strategies at the local level. *Elementary School Journal, 84*(3), 391–420.

Fullan, M. (1990). Staff development, innovation and institutional development. In B. Joyce (Ed.), *Changing school culture through staff development* (pp. 3–25). Alexandria, VA: Association of Supervision and Curriculum Development.

Fullan, M. (1991). *The new meaning of educational change.* New York: Teachers College Press.

Fullan, M. (1995). The school as a learning organization: Distant dreams. *Theory Into Practice, 34*(4), 230–235.

Fullan, M. (2000, April). The three stories of education reform. *Phi Delta Kappan, 81*(8), 581–584.

Fullan, M. (2001). *The new meaning of educational change* (3rd ed.). New York: Teachers College Press.

Fullan, M. (2002). *Leadership in a culture of change.* San Francisco: Jossey-Bass.

Fullan, M., & Miles, M. (1992, June). Getting reform right: What works and what doesn't. *Phi Delta Kappan, 73*(10), 744–752.

Fullan, M. G., & Stiegelbauer, S. M. (1991). *The new meaning of educational change.* New York: Teachers College Press.

Galagan, P. (1994, December). Reinventing the profession. *Training and Development, 48*(12), 20–27.

Gardner, J. W. (1990). *On leadership*. New York: Free Press.

Getzels, J. W., Lipham, J., & Campbell, R. (1968). *Educational administration as a social process*. New York: Harper and Row.

Glickman, C. D. (2002). *Leadership for learning*. Alexandria, VA: Association for Supervision and Curriculum Development.

Gordon, S. (1991). *How to help beginning teachers succeed*. Alexandria, VA: Association for Supervision and Curriculum Development.

Guskey, T. R. (2000). *Evaluating professional development*. Thousand Oaks, CA: Corwin Press.

Guskey, T. R., & Peterson, K. D. (1993). The road to classroom change. *Educational Leadership, 53*(4), 10–14.

Hacker, S. K., & Willard, M. L. (2002). *The trust imperative: Performance improvement through productive relationships*. Milwaukee, WI: Quality Press.

Hall, G. E., & Hord, S. M. (1987). *Change in schools: Facilitating the process*. Albany: State University of New York Press.

Hansen, J. M., & Smith, R. (1989). Building-based instructional improvement: The principal as instructional leader. *NASSP Bulletin, 73*(5), 10–16.

Hargreaves, A. (1995, April). Renewal in the age of paradox. *Educational Leadership, 52*(7), 14–19.

Hart, A. W., & Murphy, M. J. (1990). New teachers react to redesigned teacher work. *American Journal of Education, 98*(3), 224–250.

Havelock, R. G. (1971). *Planning for innovation through dissemination and utilization of knowledge*. Ann Arbor: University of Michigan, Institute for Social Research.

Hawley, W. D., & Valli, L. (1999). The essentials of effective professional development: A new consensus. In L. Darling-Hammond and G. Sykes (Eds.), *Teaching as the learning profession* (pp. 127–150). San Francisco: Jossey-Bass.

Hipp, K. A. (1997). *Documenting the effects of transformational leadership behavior on teacher efficacy*. Paper presented at the annual meeting of the American Educational Research Association, Chicago.

Hipp, K. A., & Huffman, J. B. (2000). How leadership is shared and visions emerge in the creation of learning communities. In P. Jenlink & T. Kowalski (Eds.), *Marching into a new millennium: Challenges to educational leadership* (pp. 228–309). Lanham, MD: Scarecrow Press.

Hipp, K. A., & Huffman, J. B. (2002). *Documenting and examining practices in creating learning communities: Exemplars and non-exemplars.* Paper presented at the annual meeting of the American Educational Research Association, New Orleans, LA.

Hoerr, T. R. (1996). Collegiality: A new way to define instructional leadership. *Phi Delta Kappan, 77*(5), 380–381.

Hord, S. M. (1997a). *Professional learning communities: Communities of continuous inquiry and improvement*. Austin, TX: Southwest Educational Development Laboratory.

Hord, S. M. (1997b). Professional learning communities: What are they and why are they important? *Issues about Change, 6*(1), Austin, TX: Southwest Educational Development Laboratory, 1–8.

Hord, S. M. (1998). *School professional staff as learning community*. Austin, TX: Southwest Educational Development Laboratory.

Hord, S., Chapman, R., Hinson, R. G., Hipp, K. A., Jacoby, C. L., Huffman, J. B., Pankake, A. M., Sattes, B., Thomas, J. J., & Westbrook, J. (2000). *Multiple mirrors: Reflections on the creation of professional learning communities.* Austin, TX: Southwest Educational Development Laboratory.

Hord, S. M., Meehan, M. L., Orletsky, S., & Sattes, B. (1999). Assessing a school staff as a community of professional learners. *Issues about Change, 7*(1), 1–8.

Hord, S. M., Rutherford, W. L., Huling-Austin, L., & Hall, G. E. (1987). *Taking charge of change*. Alexandria, VA: Association for Supervision and Curriculum Development.

House, E. R. (1981). Three perspectives in innovation. In R. Lehming and M. Kane (Eds.), *Improving schools: Using what we know* (pp. 17–41). Beverly Hills, CA: Sage.

Hoy, W. K., & Hannum, J. W. (1997). Middle school climate: an empirical assessment of organizational health and student achievement. *Educational Administration Quarterly, 33*(3), 290–311.

Huffman, J. B., Hipp, K. A., Moller, G., & Pankake, A. M. (2001). Professional learning communities: Leadership, integrated, vision-directed decision making, and job embedded staff development. *Journal of School Leadership, 11*(5), 448–463.

James, W. (1958). *Talks to teachers: On psychology and to students on some of life's ideals.* New York: W.W. Norton & Company.

Johnson, S. M. (1996). *Leading to change*. San Francisco: Jossey-Bass.

Katzenmeyer, M., & Moller, G. (1996). *Awakening the sleeping giant*. Thousand Oaks, CA: Corwin Press.

Katzenmeyer, M., & Moller, G. (2001). *Awakening the sleeping giant: Leadership development for teachers* (2nd ed.). Thousand Oaks, CA: Corwin Press.

Klein-Kracht, P. A. (1993). The principal in a community of learning. *Journal of School Leadership, 3*(4), 391–399.

Kopack Hill, B. (2002). *The birth of a sustainable learning organization.* Unpublished doctoral dissertation, Cardinal Stritch University, Milwaukee, WI.

Kotter, J. P. (1990, May–June). What leaders really do. *Harvard Business Review*, 3–11.

Kowalski, T. J. (1995). *Case studies on educational administration* (2nd ed.). White Plains, NY: Longman.

Lambert, L. (1998). *Building leadership capacity in schools*. Alexandria, VA: Association for Supervision and Curriculum Development.

Larsen, M. L., & Malen, B. (1997). *The elementary school principal's influence on teachers' curricular and instructional decisions*. Paper presented at the annual meeting of the American Educational Research Association, Chicago.

Lashway, L. (1998). *Creating a learning organization*. ERIC Digest 121. (OERI RR93002006). Eugene, OR: Clearinghouse on Educational Management.

Leithwood, K., Jantzi, D., & Steinbach, R. (1995, April). *An organizational learning perspective on school responses to central policy initiatives*. Paper presented at the annual meeting of the American Educational Research Association, San Francisco.

Leithwood, K., Leonard, L., & Sharratt, L. (1997). *Conditions fostering organizational learning in schools*. Paper presented at the annual meeting of the International Congress on School Effectiveness and Improvement, Memphis, TN.

Leithwood, K., & Montgomery, D. (1982). The role of the elementary school principal in program improvement. *Review of Educational Research, 52*(3), 309–399.

Leithwood, K. A. (1992). The move towards transformational leadership. *Educational Leadership, 49*(5), 8–12.

Levy, J., & Levy, M. (1993). From chaos to community at work. In K. Gozdz (Ed.), *Community-building: Renewing spirit and learning* (pp. 105–115). San Francisco: Newleader Press.

Lewis, A. (1989). *Restructuring America's schools*. Arlington, VA: American Association of School Administrators.

Lezotte, L. W., & Bancroft, B. A. (1985, March). Growing use of effective schools model for school improvement. *Educational Leadership, 38*(7), 583–586.

Lieberman, A. (1992). Teacher leadership: What are we learning? In C. Livingston (Ed.), *Teachers as leaders: Evolving roles* (pp. 159–165). Washington, DC: National Education Association.

Lieberman, A. (1995). Restructuring schools: The dynamics of changing practice, structure, and culture. In A. Lieberman (Ed.), *The work of restructuring schools: Building from the ground up* (pp. 1–17). New York: Teachers College Press.

Lieberman, A., Falk, B., & Alexander, L. (1995). A culture in the making: Leadership in learner-centered schools. In J. Oakes & K. H. Quartz (Eds.), *Creating new educational communities*: *Ninety-fourth yearbook of the National Society for the Student of Education* (pp. 108–129). Chicago: University of Chicago Press.

Lieberman, A., & Miller, L. (1981). Synthetic of research on improving schools. *Educational Leadership, 42*(6), 23–27.

Lindle, J. C. (1995/1996). Lessons from Kentucky about school-based decision making. *Educational Leadership, 35*(4), 20–23.

Little, J. W. (1981). *School success and staff development in urban segregated schools*. Paper presented at the annual meeting of the Southwest Educational Research Association, Dallas.

Little, J. W. (1997). *Excellence in professional development and professional community*. Washington, DC: Office of Educational Research and Improvement.

Louis, K. S., & Kruse, S. D. (1995). *Professionalism and community*: Perspectives on reforming urban schools. Thousand Oaks, CA: Corwin Press.

Louis, K. S., Kruse, S. D., & Marks, H. M. (1996). Schoolwide professional community. In F. Newmann and Associates (Eds.), *Authentic Achievement: Restructuring Schools for Intellectual Quality*. San Francisco: Jossey-Bass.

Louis, K. S., & Marks, H. M. (1996). *Does professional community affect the classroom teacher's work and student experiences in restructuring schools*? Paper presented at the annual meeting of the American Educational Research Association, New York.

McLaughlin, M. (1993). What matters most in teachers' workplace context. In J. W. Little & M. McLaughlin (Eds.), *Teachers' work: Individuals, colleagues, and context*. New York: Teachers College Press.

McLaughlin, M. W., & Talbert, J. E. (1993). *Contexts that matter for teaching and learning*. Stanford, CA: Center for Research on the Context of Secondary School Teaching, Stanford University.

Midgley, C., & Wood, S. (1993, November). Beyond site-based management: Empowering teachers to reform schools. *Phi Delta Kappan, 75*(3), 245–252.

Mitchell, C., & Sackney, L. (2000). Profound improvement: Building capacity for a learning community. Lisse, NL: Swets & Zeitlinger.

Mitchell, C., & Sackney, L. (2001). *Communities of learners: Developing leadership capacity for a learning community.* Paper presented at the annual conference of the American Educational Research Association, Seattle, WA.

Moore, S., & Shaw, P. (2000). *The professional learning needs and perceptions of secondary school teachers: Implications for a professional learning community*. Paper presented at the annual meeting of the American Educational Research Association, New Orleans, LA.

Morrisey, M. S. (2000). *Professional learning communities: An ongoing exploration*. Austin, TX: Southwest Educational Development Laboratory.

Mortimore, P., & Sammons, P. (1987). New evidence on effective elementary schools. *Educational Leadership, 45*(1), 4–8.

Muncey, D. E., & McQuillan, P. J. (1993). Preliminary findings from a five-year study of the Coalition of Essential Schools. *Phi Delta Kappan, 74*(6), 486–489.

National Commission of Excellence in Education. (1983). *A nation at risk: The imperative for educational reform.* Washington, DC: U.S. Government Printing Office.

National Commission on Teaching and America's Future (NCTAF) (1996). *What matters most: Teaching for America's future.* New York: Authors.

National Education Association (1993). *It's about time.* Washington, DC: Authors.

National Education Commission on Time and Learning (1994). *Prisoners of time.* Washington, DC: U. S. Government Printing Office.

National Staff Development Council (2001). *Standards for staff development.* Oxford, OH: Authors.

Newmann, F. M. (1999). We can't get there from here: Critical issues in school reform. *Phi Delta Kappan, 80*(4), 288–294.

Newmann, F. M., & Wehlage, G. (1995). *Successful school restructuring.* Madison, WI: Center on Organization and Restructuring of Schools, School of Education, University of Wisconsin–Madison.

Olivier, D. F., Cowan, D., & Pankake, A. (2000). *Professional learning communities: Cultural characteristics.* Paper presented at the annual meeting of the Southwest Educational Research Association, Dallas, TX.

Olivier, D. F., Hipp, K. K., & Huffman, J. B. (in press, 2003). Professional learning community assessment. In J. B. Huffman & K. K. Hipp (Eds.), *Professional learning communities: Initiation to implementation* (pp. 133–141, 171–173). Lanham, MD: Scarecrow Press.

Ovando, M. N. (1994). *Effects of teachers' leadership on their teaching practices.* Paper presented at the annual conference of the University Council of Educational Administration, Philadelphia.

Peterson, P. L., McCarthy, S. J., & Elmore, R. F. (1996, Spring). Learning from school restructuring. *American Educational Research Journal, 33*(1), 119–153.

Prestine, N. A. (1993). Extending the essential schools metaphor: Principal as enabler. *Journal of School Leadership, 3*(4), 356–379.

Purnell, S., & Hill, P. (1992). *Time for reform.* Santa Monica, CA: Rand Corporation.

Richmond, T. (2002). *Leadership expert Ronald Heifetz.* Retrieved September 17, 2002, from www.inc.com/magazine/19881001/5990.html.

Ridley, K. (2002, September/October). Tracking the glimmer. *Hope Magazine*, 3.

Rosenholtz, S. J. (1989). *Teachers' workplace: The social organization of schools.* New York: Longman.

Rost, J. C. (1993). *Leadership for the twenty-first century.* Westport, CT: Praeger.

Rutherford, W. L., Hord, S. M., Huling, L., & Hall, G. E. (1983). *Change facilitators: In search of understanding their role.* Austin, TX: The University of Texas, Research and Development Center for Teacher Education.

Sackney, L., Shakotko, D., Walker, K., & Hajnal, V. (1998). *Successful and unsuccessful institutionalization of school improvement.* Presented by L. Sackney to International Congress of School Improvement and Effectiveness, Manchester, England, January 5.

Sashkin, M., & Egermeier, J. (1992). *School change models and processes: A review of research and practice.* Paper presented at the annual meeting of the American Educational Research Association, San Francisco.

Schlechty, P. (1997). *Inventing better schools.* San Francisco: Jossey-Bass.

Schmitt, M. T. (2002). *Documenting the experience of a public high school in building and sustaining a professional learning community.* Unpublished doctoral dissertation, Cardinal Stritch University, Milwaukee, WI.

Senge, P. M. (1990). *The fifth discipline: The art and practice of the learning organization.* New York: Currency Doubleday.

Sergiovanni, T. J. (1992). *Moral leadership: Getting to the heart of school improvement.* San Francisco: Jossey-Bass.

Sergiovanni, T. J. (1994). *Building community in schools.* San Francisco: Jossey-Bass.

Shields, P. M., & Knapp, M. S. (1997). The promise and limits of school-based reform: A national snapshot. *Phi Delta Kappan, 79*(4), 288–294.

Short, P. M. (1994). Defining teacher empowerment. *Education, 114*(4), 488–492.

Silins, H., Mulford, B., & Zarins, S. (1999). *Leadership for organizational learning and student outcomes. The LOLSO Project: The first report of an Australian three-year study of international significance.* Paper presented at the annual meeting of the American Educational Research Association, Montreal, Canada.

Sirotnik, K. A. (1989). The school as the center of change. In T. J. Sergiovanni & H. H. Moore (Eds.), *Schooling for tomorrow: Directing reforms to issues that count.* Boston: Allyn & Bacon.

Smith, P. A., Hoy, W. A., & Sweetland, S. R. (2001, March). Organizational health of high schools and dimensions of faculty trust. *Journal of School Leadership, 11*(2), 135–151.

Smith, W. F., & Andrews, R. L. (1989). *Instructional leadership: How principals make a difference.* Alexandria, VA: Association for Supervision and Curriculum Development.

Snyder, K. J., Acker-Hocevar, M., & Snyder, K. M. (1996, Winter). Principals speak out on changing school work cultures. *Journal of Staff Development, 17*(1), 14–19.

Sparks, D. (1999). Real-life view: Here's what a true learning community looks like. *Journal of Staff Development, 204*(4), 53–57.

Spaulding, A. M. (1994). *The politics of the principal: Influencing teachers' school-based decision making*. Paper presented at the annual meeting of the American Educational Research Association, New Orleans, LA.

Stein, M. K. (1998). *High-performance learning communities District 2: Report on year-one implementation of school learning communities*. High-performance training communities project. Washington, DC: ERIC (ERIC Document Reproduction Service No. ED429263).

Svec, V., Pourdavood, R. G., & Cowen, L. M. (1999). *Challenges of instructional leadership for reforming school*. Paper presented at the annual meeting of the American Educational Research Association, Montreal, Canada.

Tarter, C. J., Sabo, D., & Hoy, W. K. (1995). Middle school climate, faculty trust, and effectiveness: A path analysis. *Journal of Research and Development in Education, 29*(1), 41–49.

Texas Education Agency (2002). *No child left behind*. Retrieved May 2002 from www.tea.state.tx.us.

Thomas, M. (1978). A study of alternative views. *American Education: Vol. 2. The role of the principal*. Santa Monica, CA: RAND.

Wagner, T. (1998, March). Change as collaborative inquiry: A constructivist methodology for reinventing schools. *Phi Delta Kappan*, 512–517.

Walker, D. (2002). Contructivist leadership: Standards, equity, and learning—Weaving Whole cloth from multiple strands. In D. Walker, J. E. Cooper, D. P. Zimmerman, M. D. Lambert, M. E. Gardner, P. J. Ford Slack, L. Lambert, M. Lambert Zimmerman, & J. E. Cooper (Eds.), *The constructivist leader* (2nd ed.) (pp. 1–33). New York: Teachers College Press.

Walker, K., & Sackney, L. (1999). *Learning communities as substitute for school accountability*. Paper presented at the University Council for Educational Administration, Minneapolis, MN.

Weller, L. D., & Weller, S. J. (1997, October). Quality learning organizations and continuous improvement: Implementing the concept. *NAAPS Bulletin, 81*(591), 62–70.

Wheatley, M. J. (1994). *Leadership and the new science: Learning about organization from an orderly universe*. San Francisco: Berrett-Koehler.

Whyte, D. (1994). *The heart aroused: Poetry and the preservation of the soul in corporate America*. New York: Currency Doubleday.

Whyte, D. (2001). *Crossing the unknown sea: Work as a pilgrim of identity.* New York: Riverhead Books.

Wignall, R. (1992). *Building a collaborative school culture: A case study of one woman in the principalship.* Paper presented at the European Conference on Educational Research, Enschede, The Netherlands.

Wood, F. H., & Killian, J. (1998). Job-embedded learning makes the difference in school improvement. *Journal of Staff Development, 19*(1), 52–54.

Wood, F. H., & McQuarrie, F., Jr. (1999). On-the-job learning. *The Journal of Staff Development, 20*(3), 10–13.

Zempke, R. (1999, September). Why organizations still aren't learning. *Training, 36*(9), 40–42, 44, 46, 49.

Zinn, L. F. (1997). *Supports and barriers to teacher leadership: Reports of teacher leaders.* Paper presented at the annual meeting of the American Educational Research Association, Chicago.

Index

About the Authors

Jane Bumpers Huffman is an associate professor in the College of Education at the University of North Texas in Denton, and teaches in the master's and doctoral programs. Dr. Huffman also serves as her department's program coordinator for educational administration and has been instrumental in receiving eight grants. Her research interests include change management, professional development, leadership, professional learning communities, and parent involvement. Dr. Huffman has also directed the annual Assistant Principals' Conference in Texas for the past six years. She holds a bachelor's degree in education, a master's degree in social sciences, and a doctoral degree in administration, curriculum, and supervision from the University of Oklahoma. Her graduate work focused on staff development and the achievement of school goals. Dr. Huffman worked in the Norman, Oklahoma, public schools for 10 years as a teacher, school administrator, and staff development administrator. She also served as a research assistant at Southwest Educational Development Laboratory in Austin, Texas. Contact Dr. Huffman at huffman@unt.edu or 940-565-2832.

Kristine Kiefer Hipp is an associate professor in the College of Education at Cardinal Stritch University, Milwaukee, Wisconsin. She teaches in a master's program in educational leadership and a doctoral program in leadership for the advancement of learning and service. Dr. Hipp consults widely, facilitating organizational change in K–12 schools/districts related to her research in leadership, professional learning communities, and collective efficacy. She holds bachelor's and master's degrees in special education from the University of Wisconsin–Whitewater and a doctoral degree in educational administration from the University of Wisconsin–Madison. Her doctoral work focused on the relationship of transformational leadership behavior and teacher efficacy. Dr. Hipp also taught in a master's program in educational leadership at Ball State University in Muncie, Indiana. She worked for the school district of Janesville for 25 years as a special education teacher/support teacher, district-level staff developer, graduate-level adjunct at the University of Wisconsin–Whitewater, research assistant at the University of Wisconsin–Madison, and consultant in effective teaching practices. Contact Dr. Hipp at kahipp@stritch.edu or 414-410-4346.

The authors have presented their research at the local, state, national, and international levels, and published articles in national and international refereed journals and book chapters. Dr. Huffman and Dr. Hipp have collaborated as part of a research team and have coauthored extensively over the past four years on papers presented at the American Educational Research Association (AERA) and publications in the *Journal of School Leadership*, the *International Journal of Educational Reform*, the *Eighth Yearbook of the National Council of Professors of Educational Administration*, and *Planning and Changing*. Samples of their work include:

- *An International Perspective on the Development of Learning Communities*
- *Professional Learning Communities: Development—Assessment—Effects*
- *How Leadership is Shared and Visions Emerge in the Creation of Learning Communities*
- *Documenting and Examining Practices in Creating Learning Communities: Exemplars and Non-Exemplars*
- *Professional Learning Communities: Leadership, Integrated, Vision-Directed Decision Making, and Job Embedded Staff Development*
- *Creating Communities of Learners: The Interaction of Shared Leadership, Shared Vision, and Supportive Conditions*
- *Two Professional Learning Communities: Tales from the Field*

About the Contributors

Anita M. Pankake is professor of educational administration at Texas Pan American, Edinburg, Texas. Her bachelor's and master's degrees are from Indiana State University, Terre Haute, Indiana; her doctorate is from Loyola University–Chicago. Prior to her work in higher education she served as a teacher, assistant principal, and principal in Indiana and Illinois. She has authored and coauthored numerous articles in the areas of leadership, organizational change, and professional development. She coauthored *The Effective Elementary Principal* with I. Emett Burnett, Jr., Ph.D., and is the author of *Implementation: Making Things Happen*, Eye on Education. *Implementation* received the Outstanding Publication Award for 2000 from the Texas Staff Development Council.

Gayle Moller is an assistant professor in the Department of Educational Leadership and Foundations in the College of Education and Allied Professions at Western Carolina University in Cullowhee, North Carolina. She was formerly executive director of the South Florida Center for Educational Leaders. Gayle worked in the Broward County public schools for 19 years as a teacher, school administrator, and staff development administrator. She received her doctorate from Teachers College/Columbia University. Her graduate work centered on staff development for shared decision making. Teacher leadership, professional development, and professional learning communities are her research interests. She is the coauthor, with Marilyn Katzenmeyer, of

Awakening the Sleeping Giant: Helping Teachers Develop as Leaders, 2nd edition.

D'Ette Fly Cowan is a program associate at the Southwest Educational Development Laboratory in Austin, Texas. She holds a bachelor's degree in education from the University of Texas at Austin, a master's degree in reading from Baylor University, and a Doctor of Education degree in educational administration from the University of Texas at Austin. Previously, she has served in Texas as a consultant for a regional service center, an elementary school principal, and a junior high school reading teacher. Her research interests are school leadership, comprehensive school improvement, and qualitative research.

Dianne F. Olivier is the director of curriculum and instruction for St. Martin Parish School System, Louisiana. She holds a bachelor's and a master's degree in education and an educational specialist degree in administration and supervision from the University of Southwestern Louisiana. She holds a Doctor of Philosophy degree in educational leadership and administration from Louisiana State University, with a minor in psychology. She has 30-plus years in public school education, with over 20 years in administration. Dianne is an adjunct faculty member for Louisiana State University. Her research interests are school culture, teacher self and collective efficacy, and professional learning communities.